LIGHT
PASTA SAUCES

MAGGIE RAMSAY

PHOTOGRAPHS BY
ROBIN MATTHEWS

RIZZOLI
NEW YORK

CONTENTS

INTRODUCTION

Light pasta sauces? Surely pasta was made to welcome cream, cheese, olive oil, and butter? What can compare with the comfort of a creamy carbonara sauce, the richness of pesto, or the wonderful aroma of garlic sizzling in olive oil or butter? Of course, it would be nutritionally absurd to do without fat altogether, but since so many people these days are trying to cut down on the amount of fat they eat, especially saturated fat, I've developed recipes for this book that emphasize other flavors.

None of the recipes include more than $\frac{1}{2}$ tablespoon of added oil per person. Meat, oily fish, cheese, and nuts do, of course, contain fat, but they also contribute valuable protein, vitamins, and minerals, which are essential to a healthy diet. In combination with pasta, and perhaps a side salad, most of these sauces make a complete, satisfying, and well-balanced meal.

My suggestions for specific pasta shapes to go with each sauce do not always conform to "rules" about matching pasta with sauces—sometimes the combination just felt right. It's up to you which shape you use.

More important, in some recipes I've stated "toss with" and in others "serve over" pasta. Sometimes it's worth combining the pasta with the sauce so it picks up the flavors, but on other occasions the pasta is there to provide a background color or supporting flavor, so mixing them before they land on the plate would be a mistake.

One of the great things I discovered while cooking my way through these 100 dishes is the joy of fat-free dishwashing: There are no sticky plates and pans to deal with.

So if you're looking for some healthy additions to your repertoire of pasta suppers, I hope you have as much fun cooking with this book as I did writing it.

Maggie Ramsay

Left: Avocado Salsa (page 58)

A WELL-STOCKED PANTRY

You will easily find all the ingredients used in this book in supermarkets, gourmet stores, and Oriental markets.

You don't need to rush out and buy them all, but the following selection offers some suggestions for your shopping list. The ingredients

listed under "Basics" are naturally low in fat and can be included in your diet on a regular basis. As a general rule, you can eat as

much of these as you want. Ingredients listed under "Flavorings," however, provide some of the traditional aroma and flavors

associated with pasta dishes, but should be restricted to occasional treats because of their higher fat content.

BASICS

CHILIES
There are various ways to add the hot, spicy flavor of chili to a pasta sauce. You can include fresh red or green chilies, dried whole chilies, chili flakes, cayenne pepper, and hot pepper sauces, or add an Asian influence with bottled chili-garlic sauce and sweet chili sauce. In some recipes it doesn't matter which you use; in others fresh chilies are essential to add a splash of color as well as flavor.

GARLIC
Garlic is a versatile flavoring that appears many pasta sauces. It can be simmered, baked, roasted, used raw, or quickly stir-fried. How much you add is really up to you. If a recipe says 2 or 3 cloves, it means 2 large or 3 small cloves.

HERBS
Some dried herbs such as oregano, thyme, and bay leaves are useful as seasonings, but to add a vibrant flavor and a splash of color, I use fresh herbs in many sauces.

LEMONS, LIMES, ORANGES
The tang of citrus juice lifts and enlivens sauces; and just a squeeze of fresh juice can do the trick. Pared zest in fine strips adds flavor and color, which is why I often include it as a low-fat garnish.

MIRIN AND SAKE
These are Japanese rice wines: Sake is dry, mirin sweet.

MUSHROOMS
When choosing fresh mushrooms, remember button and oyster mushrooms keep their pale color during cooking, so they are best to include in delicate and fish sauces, while cremini and shiitake mushrooms will inevitably darken a sauce, ideal for meat- and lentil-based sauces.

A package of dried porcini (cep or *Boletus edulis*) is always useful to keep in stock. They keep for up to a year, and add a wonderful fragrance and intense flavor to mushroom sauces. To use, soak in warm water for 30 minutes before straining and adding to the sauce.

PASTA
Few kitchen pantries are without dried pasta. It's a versatile, low-fat, low-sodium ingredient that contains varying amounts of valuable vitamins and other nutrients, especially if you use an enriched brand. Wholewheat pastas are also an excellent source of dietary fiber. The key to keeping pasta low fat and giving it a significant role in a healthy diet is not to top it with a rich, fatty sauce.

The choice of shapes is almost limitless. I give suggestions with each recipe, but feel free to use whatever shape you like.

SPICES
Keep spices in airtight jars in a cool pantry. Some useful ones are paprika, saffron strands, ground cinnamon, and ground cumin. Ground spices soon lose their fragrance, so buy in small quantities and throw away old packages.

TAMARI
This is Japanese soy sauce, brewed without chemical additives or wheat. Used as a seasoning, it complements pasta and all sorts of vegetables. However, it does darken sauces.

TOFU
Popular in Asia, especially Japan, white tofu is made from curdled soy milk, which is extracted from cooked soybeans. Although bland, it is able to absorb the flavor of the food with which it is cooked. Tofu is also available smoked, which has more flavor.

Tofu has the advantages of being low in calories, high in protein, and cholesterol-free. Store for up to a week in the refrigerator, or freeze for up to 3 months.

TOMATOES
Fresh tomatoes are the archetypal partner for pasta. They must smell good when you buy them, otherwise you are wasting your money—bland, watery, or woolly-textured tomatoes will spoil any dish.

Canned chopped tomatoes are the basis of many a low-fat pasta sauce.

"Passata" means sieved in Italian and refers to a smooth tomato puree, sold in jars in Italian delicatessens.

Sun-dried tomatoes will last for up to a year in your pantry, ready to add extra flavor to sauces.

Tomato paste adds concentrated tomato flavor where you don't need the bulk of tomatoes. Keep a tube or can in the refrigerator.

YOGURT
Use low-fat plain yogurt as an alternative to cream, but do not cook it over direct heat unless you stablize it first with cornstarch.

FLAVORINGS

ANCHOVIES
Available preserved in salt or oil; these should be rinsed before using. Pat dry with paper towels.

MUSTARD
I use a small amount of coarse Dijon mustard to add flavor to some sauces.

NUTS
Although these are high in fat, it is mainly of the unsaturated kind, and they are packed with vitamins and minerals, so I have included almonds, pine nuts, pistachios, and walnuts in sauces that are otherwise very low in fat.

OILS
All oils are equally high in fat but most vegetable oils have a reasonably low proportion of saturated fat. For general cooking I use peanut or sunflower oil. Using a nonstick pan is one easy way to reduce the amount of oil you use. Another trick is to warm the pan *before* you add any oil.

Olive: Olive oil is suggested in recipes where its flavor is a feature of the dish. You won't be using much, so buy the best extra-virgin olive oil you can afford.

Truffle: Truffle oil is expensive, but you need only a few drops on hot pasta to add an incomparable aroma. Look for it in gourmet stores.

Sesame: Sesame oil is inexpensive and available in supermarkets and Chinese markets. Again, you need only a few drops at the last minute.

OLIVES
Olives are sold packed in oil or brine, and in this book I specify the brined variety to keep the fat content as low as possible.

PANCETTA
It really is worth going to a good Italian delicatessen to buy this delicious, unsmoked Italian bacon cured with salt and spices. Well wrapped, it will keep for 3 weeks in the refrigerator. You don't need much to give a dish a pronounced flavor, and it doesn't collapse during cooking.

PROSCIUTTO
This cured ham, of which Parma ham is only one type, is usually sold thinly sliced. The fat is clearly visible, so you can cut off as much as you want to reduce the fat content of the dish.

SAUCES
Some prepared sauces are excellent flavor boosters. These include chili-garlic sauce, hoisin sauce, hot pepper sauce, soy sauce and tamari (see page 7), Thai fish sauce (called *nam pla* in Thailand; *nuoc mam* in Vietnam), and Worcestershire sauce. You must read the labels carefully, however, because despite being low fat most are high in sodium, which many people try to avoid or reduce.

TECHNIQUES

The most valuable advice I can give is to read a recipe through before you attempt to cook it. It will also save time if you measure the ingredients and do all the preparation in advance, then you can just cook your way through the recipe without stopping.

COOKING PASTA
Despite a popular misconception, it is not necessary to add a tablespoon of oil to the cooking water to prevent pasta sticking together. Instead, just make sure you use a large saucepan and plenty of water. If there is not enough water, the starch from the pasta will create a gluey soup. Bring the water to a steady, rolling boil, then add the pasta and 1 tablespoon salt for every 3 quarts water to bring out the flavor of the pasta. Adjust the heat to keep the

water boiling steadily, so the bubbles of the boiling water—plus an occasional stir—keep the pasta moving, preventing it from sticking together. Timing varies greatly according to the freshness and shape of the pasta. Fresh angel-hair pasta, for example, cooks in about a minute, whereas dried wholewheat spaghetti can take up to 15 minutes. Farfalle can take even longer, because the middle part where the four layers of pasta are squeezed together can remain hard when the edges are cooked.

Take care not to overcook pasta—it should have a firm, lively texture and is never meant to lie in a limp, soggy pool on the plate. Test the pasta at least a minute before the shortest time suggested on the package and keep testing every 30 seconds after that. To test, fish a piece of pasta out of the boiling water and bite it—if it has lost its chalky middle, it is ready to drain and serve. The phrase often used is *al dente*, meaning firm to the bite.

As soon as the pasta is cooked it must be drained in a colander. Shake the colander firmly to remove excess water, but you don't need to remove every drop; some sauces, particularly if they are thick, benefit from a little of the pasta cooking water. Quickly toss the pasta with the sauce or transfer it to a warmed serving dish and pour the sauce over it.

PASTA QUANTITIES
Depending on your appetite and the other dishes in the meal, allow 2 to 3½ ounces of dried pasta per person.

COOKING THE SAUCES
Don't be afraid to add a splash of water (preferably the pasta cooking water) if your sauce is too thick, is boiling too rapidly, or looks likely to stick to the pan.

SKINNING AND SEEDING TOMATOES
Remove the stems. Cut a small "x" in the bottom of each tomato and place in a heatproof bowl. Pour boiling water over the tomatoes and leave for 10 to 15 seconds. Drain and immediately return the tomatoes to the bowl and cover them with cold water, then drain again. The skins should peel away easily. Slice the tomatoes in half around the middle and scoop out the seeds with a teaspoon.

ROASTING AND SKINNING PEPPERS
Heat the oven to its highest setting. Roast the peppers in a roasting pan or baking dish until the skins turn black, about 20 minutes. Put them in a plastic bag, seal, and leave until cool enough to handle. Peel off the charred skins, holding the peppers over a plate to collect the delicious juices. Slice in half and scoop out the seeds with a teaspoon.

PREPARING ARTICHOKE BOTTOMS
Choose fresh-looking green or purple-tinged globe artichokes; reject withered, brown ones. Soak them upside-down in a bowl of cold, salted water for an hour. Rub a halved lemon over the cut surfaces of the artichokes as you work to prevent them from discoloring. Snap off the stem and pull off the outer leaves. Slice across the top and pull out the central leaves. Finally, scrape out the hairy "choke" from the middle—a teaspoon is the best tool for this.

CLEANING MUSSELS
Mussels can be very gritty, even if they look clean on the outside. The following method removes as much grit as possible:

Rinse the mussels thoroughly, scrubbing the shells and discarding any broken mussels and any open ones that do not close when tapped. Put the mussels in a large bowl of clean water with a good spoonful of sea salt and swirl them around. Leave them to soak for at least 2 hours, changing the water four or five times. This may sound like a lot of fuss but it's not difficult to do, and when the mussels are clean they are incredibly quick to cook.

CLEANING SQUID
Pull the tentacles away from the body tube, cut off the tentacles just below the eyes, and discard any hard parts. Pull out and discard the transparent backbone from inside the body tube. Rinse the squid briefly, then rub off any purplish skin.

UTENSILS

You will probably own most of the utensils listed below already. Some are everyday kitchen items; others, although not essential, will help you create pasta sauces quickly and easily. Top of the list is a large saucepan with a 4-quart capacity for cooking the pasta.

LARGE COLANDER
This is essential for draining pasta. Choose a sturdy stainless steel or enamel one with a flat bottom so that you can put it in the sink to drain the pasta as soon as it's done.

HEAVY-BOTTOMED SAUCEPAN AND SKILLET
Stainless steel or enamel cast-iron pans for cooking sauces need thick bottoms to spread the heat evenly. This helps prevent ingredients from sticking and burning.

WOK
A wok is useful for stir-frying sauces over high heat. If you don't have one, just use a large, deep skillet.

RIDGED GRILL PAN
Heavy ridged pans can be heated to a high temperature, then brushed lightly with oil to cook meat, fish, and vegetables quickly, giving them a distinctive chargrilled flavor. If you don't have one, use your broiler—again, heat it to a high temperature first—and brush the broiler rack with a light coating of oil.

MEASURING CUP
A clearly marked heatproof measuring cup is useful for both measuring and mixing liquids.

CHOPPING BOARDS
Wooden or acrylic boards protect your work surfaces, knives, and fingers. Avoid hard, melamine boards because they blunt knives and worse, can cause them to slip.

MEZZALUNA
This half-moon or rocking chopper is excellent for mincing herbs, garlic, anchovies and other small ingredients. Most are sold with a concave chopping board.

MORTAR AND PESTLE
Some herb and spice mixtures are best crushed together in a mortar. Choose a heavy stone pestle to make the job as easy as possible.

BLENDER
Pureeing mixtures in a blender produces a smooth sauce; this is essential in some of the recipes.

FOOD PROCESSOR
Chopping and slicing large quantities of vegetables is easy with a food processor. It can also help to make certain sauces.

RUBBER SPATULA
Invaluable for scraping down the sides of the blender or food processor.

LEMON ZESTER
This handy little tool is far more effective than a regular grater for paring off neat strips of lemon, lime, or orange zest to flavor or garnish a dish.

DRAINING SPOON
Choose a slotted spoon with small holes to lift ingredients out of a liquid sauce.

WOODEN SPAGHETTI SERVER
Long pasta such as spaghetti can tangle into a solid bird's nest in the pan, and a spaghetti server helps you separate it into individual portions.

KNIVES, BOWLS, SPOONS, AND SPATULAS
Does any kitchen not have these? Ideally there will be two or three of each: Knives must be sharp for efficient chopping; toughened glass bowls in different sizes can be used for mixing and storing; long-handled wooden spoons and spatulas are easier on your pans than metal ones.

THE RECIPES

FAST & EASY

When you want a quick and easy supper dish that consists mostly of ingredients likely to be in your pantry already with only one or two fresh items to purchase, this is the chapter for you. As a bonus, most of the sauces are cooked in only one or two pans to save on clean up.

FISH WITH PIMENTOS, PINE NUTS, AND PARSLEY

Use any firm-fleshed white fish that won't break up in the pan, such as swordfish or sea bass. Canned red bell peppers make this a speedy dish. Alternatively, use four roasted and skinned peppers (see page 9). Any shape of pasta is suitable.

1 pound fish fillets
1 tablespoon olive oil
Salt and freshly ground black pepper
2 garlic cloves, minced

1 can (14-oz.) red pimentos, drained and cut into strips
4 tablespoons pine nuts, lightly toasted
4 tablespoons chopped fresh parsley

Brush the fish lightly with the oil and season with salt and pepper; set aside.

Heat a heavy-bottomed skillet until it is very hot. Sear the fish in the hot pan for 1 to 2 minutes on each side until just cooked through. Remove from the pan; keep warm.

Add the garlic and pimento strips to the pan and heat through. Add the pine nuts and parsley and season with salt and pepper to taste. Toss with hot pasta. Serve the fish on top.

GOLDEN ONION AND ANCHOVY

Combining the sweetness of onions and the saltiness of anchovies, this is a satisfying sauce for anchovy lovers—use a half can of anchovies to make a single portion. This sauce is ideal to serve with orecchiette.

1½ tablespoons olive oil
4 onions, thinly sliced
2 garlic cloves, sliced

2 cans (2-oz.) anchovy fillets, rinsed (see page 7) and chopped
Freshly ground black pepper

Warm a heavy-bottomed saucepan over the stove; reduce the heat to low and add the oil. Add the onions and stir to coat in the oil. Cover the pan tightly so the onions cook in their own steam for about 20 minutes, uncovering and stirring from time to time to prevent them from sticking.

When the onions are soft, uncover the pan, turn up the heat, and stir more frequently until they start to turn golden brown. Add the garlic and anchovies and stir to heat through. Season with black pepper. Toss with hot pasta and serve at once.

LAMB AND MINT PESTO

The flavor of fresh mint complements both lamb and peas in this all-in-one dish. Serve with rigatoni.

1 pound lean ground lamb
1 onion, minced
2 to 3 tablespoons prepared pesto sauce

2 to 3 tablespoons finely chopped fresh mint
1½ cups fresh or frozen shelled peas
Salt and freshly ground black pepper

Warm a heavy-bottomed saucepan over the stove; reduce the heat to medium-high and add the lamb and onion. Cook over medium-high heat for 8 to 10 minutes, stirring to break up the meat.

Add all the remaining ingredients, cover, and simmer for 5 to 7 minutes, adding 1 to 2 tablespoons of the pasta cooking water if necessary to prevent sticking. Season to taste with salt and pepper and toss with hot pasta.

SCALLOPS AND LIME

Serve this delicate, tangy sauce with linguine.

¾ cup fish stock
12 large fresh scallops
1 teaspoon peeled and grated fresh ginger
1 tablespoon soy sauce, plus more if needed

2 teaspoons cornstarch, dissolved in 1 tablespoon water
Juice and zest of 1 lime, cut into thin strips
Salt (optional)

Bring the fish stock to a boil in a saucepan. Reduce the heat to low and poach the scallops in the stock for 1 to 2 minutes. Using a draining spoon, transfer the scallops to a warmed plate. Slice each scallop in half horizontally; cover and keep warm.

Add the ginger and soy sauce to the stock and bring to a boil. Remove from the heat, stir in the cornstarch, and return to a boil to thicken the sauce. Add a little lime juice, then taste the sauce and add more lime juice, soy sauce, or salt as required. Pour the sauce over hot pasta and top with the scallops and lime zest.

SMOKED CHICKEN AND LEEK WITH COARSE MUSTARD

This is a rich-tasting sauce with a fraction of the fat it would have if it was made with cream. If you can't find smoked chicken, substitute lean smoked ham. Serve with conchiglie or tagliatelle.

2 to 3 small leeks, with as much green as edible, cut into 3-inch pieces and then cut into matchsticks	2 teaspoons cornstarch dissolved in 2 tablespoons water
1 cup low-fat plain yogurt	2 to 3 teaspoons coarse mustard
	2½ cups chopped skinless smoked chicken
	Salt and freshly ground black pepper

Plunge the leeks into a saucepan of boiling water and boil for about 2 minutes, or until just tender; do not overcook. Drain well.

Put the yogurt into a heavy-bottomed saucepan. Stir the cornstarch and mustard into the yogurt. Add the chicken and leeks and stir over low heat until heated through. Season to taste with salt and pepper. Serve over hot pasta.

TUSCAN CHICKEN LIVER SAUCE

In Tuscany, a piquant chicken liver mixture is often served on crostini to nibble with drinks before dinner. Try this variation with orecchiette or conchiglie.

1 tablespoon olive oil	2 teaspoons capers, chopped
1 shallot, minced	4 anchovy fillets, rinsed (see page 7) and finely chopped
1 garlic clove, minced	
½ pound chicken livers, roughly chopped	2 tablespoons finely chopped fresh parsley, plus extra to garnish
7 tablespoons dry white wine	
1 teaspoon tomato paste	Salt and freshly ground black pepper
7 tablespoons hot chicken stock	

Warm a heavy-bottomed saucepan over the stove; reduce the heat to medium-high and add the oil, shallot, garlic, and chicken livers. Sauté over medium-high heat for 2 to 3 minutes, stirring frequently, until the livers are brown all over but still moist and pink inside. Add the wine and stir to deglaze the pan. Reduce the heat to low and let the wine simmer until most of the liquid evaporates.

Dissolve the tomato paste in the chicken stock; set aside. Mix together the capers, anchovies, and parsley and stir into the saucepan. Add the stock and heat through. Season to taste with salt and pepper. Serve over hot pasta, garnished with extra parsley.

SCALLOPS WITH SPICY LEEKS

A bed of mildly curried leeks and pasta is the perfect foil for fresh scallops. Serve with tagliatelle.

12 large fresh scallops	1 garlic clove, crushed
1½ tablespoons peanut oil	¾ teaspoon curry powder
Salt and freshly ground black pepper	6 tablespoons low-fat plain yogurt
3 cups leeks, cut into 3-inch pieces and then cut into matchsticks	

Brush the scallops with ½ tablespoon of the oil and season lightly with salt and pepper; set aside.

Warm a heavy-bottomed saucepan over the stove, then add the remaining oil. Add the leeks, garlic, and curry powder, cover the pan, and cook for about 10 minutes, stirring occasionally, until the leeks soften; add a splash or two of water if necessary to prevent sticking. Season to taste.

Warm a heavy-bottomed skillet until it is very hot. Sear the scallops in the hot pan for about 30 seconds on each side.

Toss the leeks with the yogurt and hot pasta and serve with the scallops on top.

SMOKED HADDOCK AND SPINACH

Smoked food gives an illusion of richness without added fat. Serve this with penne.

1 pound smoked haddock	2 teaspoons cornstarch, dissolved in 2 tablespoons water
1 bay leaf	
2 to 3 sprigs fresh thyme or parsley	2 teaspoons coarse mustard
1 cup milk	Freshly ground black pepper
1 cup low-fat plain yogurt	Large handful young spinach leaves, cut into ½-inch strips

Put the haddock in a skillet. Add the herbs, milk, and just enough water to cover the fish. Bring to a boil over low heat and simmer for 1 minute. Cover the pan and remove from the heat. Leave the fish to stand for 5 to 10 minutes, then discard the liquid and break the fish into pieces, removing the skin and any bones.

Put the yogurt into a heavy-bottomed saucepan. Stir the cornstarch into the yogurt with the mustard and continue stirring over low heat until thick. Add the fish and season to taste with black pepper. When the fish is heated through, stir in the spinach and toss with hot pasta.

Right: Smoked Chicken and Leek with Coarse Mustard

FENNEL AND SHRIMP

This recipe is equally delicious if you use smoked trout in place of the shrimp. Serve with tagliatelle or tagliolini.

2 fennel bulbs, about 1 pound in total, quartered, fronds reserved	1 to 2 tablespoons lemon juice
1 tablespoon olive oil	Salt and freshly ground black pepper
10 ounces shrimp, shelled	2 tablespoons snipped fresh chives

Blanch the fennel in a large saucepan of boiling water for 1 to 2 minutes. Using a draining spoon, remove the fennel; reserve the cooking water. Slice the fennel very thinly.

Warm a heavy-bottomed saucepan over the stove, then add the oil. Add the fennel, cover with a tight-fitting lid, and cook over low heat for 10 to 15 minutes until very tender. Meanwhile, cook the pasta in the reserved fennel water; drain and set aside.

Add the shrimp to the fennel, together with lemon juice and salt and pepper to taste. Stir in the chives and hot pasta and toss together. Serve garnished with the fennel fronds.

BEEF AND MUSHROOM

The mushrooms give this sauce a full, rich flavor. This takes very little time or thought to make, especially if you use a food processor to chop the mushrooms. Serve with conchiglie, lumache, or pipe rigate.

14 ounces lean ground beef	2 tablespoons soy sauce
1 onion, minced	1 garlic clove, crushed
5 cups finely chopped mushrooms	2 tablespoons brandy
1 can (14-oz.) crushed tomatoes	Salt and freshly ground black pepper
1/4 cup grated low-fat Parmesan cheese	2 tablespoons chopped fresh parsley

Warm a heavy-bottomed saucepan over the stove, then add the beef and onion. Cover and cook over medium-high heat for 5 to 7 minutes, stirring occasionally to break up the meat. Add all the remaining ingredients, except the parsley, and simmer, uncovered, for 20 to 30 minutes until the beef is cooked through and the flavors blend.

Taste and add more salt and pepper if needed. Serve over hot pasta, garnished with parsley.

CHARGRILLED SQUID WITH SESAME DRESSING

Both the squid and the dressing can be prepared a few hours in advance for a really quick finish. This makes a dramatic-looking dinner party dish served on black squid ink pasta. Although sesame seeds are high in fat, most of it is unsaturated, and they add a pleasant crunch to this sauce. They can, however, be omitted, if you prefer.

1 pound squid bodies, cleaned (see page 9)	2 teaspoons sesame oil
1 teaspoon salt	1 tablespoon sesame seeds, lightly toasted
Good pinch cayenne pepper	(optional)

FOR THE SESAME DRESSING:

1 tablespoon prepared oyster sauce	1/2 tablespoon peanut oil
1 tablespoon tamari	1/2 tablespoon sesame oil
1 tablespoon balsamic or rice vinegar	

Slit open one side of each squid body and score the inner side with parallel lines 1/2 inch apart, then score in perpendicular lines to make a crisscross pattern. If the squid are very small, leave them whole, otherwise cut them into chunks. Keep the tentacles in bunches, but cut off any hard parts.

Mix the salt, cayenne, and sesame oil together and rub into the squid. Set aside for at least 15 minutes.

Mix all the dressing ingredients together. Heat a broiler or grill pan until very hot. Broil or grill the squid for 1 to 2 minutes, turning once, until opaque. Toss hot pasta with the dressing and the toasted sesame seeds, if using, and serve at once, topped with the squid.

SQUID PROVENÇALE

A fragrant, simple supper dish that is good with conchiglie.

2 shallots, minced	1 bay leaf
1 tablespoon olive oil	2 teaspoons dried herbes de Provence
2 garlic cloves, minced	14 ounces cleaned squid (see page 9), sliced
2 tablespoons brandy	into rings
7 tablespoons dry white wine	Grated zest of 1 orange
1 can (14-oz.) crushed tomatoes	1/2 cup pitted black olives
Pinch cayenne pepper	Handful fresh basil leaves

Cook the shallots in the olive oil until soft and translucent. Add the garlic and after 20 seconds add the brandy and stir briefly. Add the wine, tomatoes, cayenne pepper, and herbs. Simmer, uncovered, for 20 minutes, or until the sauce thickens.

Add the squid and continue simmering for 2 to 3 minutes. Stir in the orange zest and olives. Serve over hot pasta, garnished with the basil leaves.

Right: Fennel and Shrimp

CHILI BEEF WITH FRESH CILANTRO

Both the chili-garlic sauce and mirin have sweetness to balance the fieriness of the chili. (Look for the sauce in the Chinese food section of the supermarket.) Serve with linguine, egg noodles, or Southeast Asian rice sticks.

1 pound sirloin steak, cut into thin strips
6 tablespoons prepared chili-garlic sauce
4 tablespoons mirin (sweet rice wine)
1 tablespoon peanut oil

2 teaspoons cornstarch, dissolved in
*   2 tablespoons water*
8 to 10 scallions, finely sliced on the
*   diagonal*
1 bunch fresh cilantro, roughly torn

Mix the beef with the chili-garlic sauce and mirin and let marinate for at least 20 minutes.

Heat the oil in a hot wok or large skillet. Add the beef and its marinade and stir-fry over high heat for 2 to 3 minutes, stirring constantly. Add the cornstarch and about 4 tablespoons of the pasta cooking water to the wok and cook for about 1 minute, until thicker. Serve over hot pasta, topped with the sliced scallions and plenty of cilantro.

PAPRIKA CHICKEN

Serve this simple, hearty supper dish with tagliatelle, accompanied by a crisp green salad or green beans.

4 skinless, boneless chicken breast halves
1 tablespoon paprika
1 tablespoon soy sauce
1 tablespoon honey

2 teaspoons cornstarch, dissolved in
*   2 tablespoons water*
1 tablespoon peanut oil
2/3 cup chicken stock, warmed
Salt and freshly ground black pepper

Cut the chicken into thin strips, about 2 x 1/2 inches. Mix the paprika, soy sauce, and honey together in a large bowl. Stir the cornstarch into the bowl. Add the chicken and let marinate for about 15 minutes.

Heat the oil in a hot wok or large skillet. Add the chicken and marinade and stir-fry for 4 to 5 minutes, gradually adding stock to prevent sticking and to make a sauce. Season to taste with salt and pepper. Serve over hot pasta.

TURKEY, PROSCIUTTO, AND SAGE

Many supermarkets sell ground turkey, making this recipe even easier. Serve with paglia e fieno (mixed yellow and green tagliolini).

14 ounces ground turkey
4 ounces prosciutto, finely chopped
8 fresh sage leaves, finely chopped,
*   or 1 teaspoon dried sage*

1/2 cup chicken stock
1/2 cup dry white wine
Salt and freshly ground black pepper

Put all the ingredients into a saucepan, cover, and simmer over low heat for 15 minutes, stirring often to break up the turkey. Adjust the seasoning if necessary. Serve over hot pasta.

ROSEMARY CHICKEN

This is fragrant and fast. You'll probably have the basic ingredients for this sauce in your pantry, so you can get this dish on the table in less than 30 minutes. Serve with casareccie or spinach tagliatelle.

2 teaspoons Dijon mustard
1 teaspoon dried oregano
2 garlic cloves, crushed
Pinch cayenne pepper
2 1/2 cups cubed, skinless chicken breast
1 sprig fresh rosemary

1 tablespoon olive oil
2/3 cup dry white wine
1 cup chicken stock
2 teaspoons cornstarch, dissolved in
*   2 tablespoons water*

Mix the mustard, oregano, garlic, and cayenne together to form a paste in a large bowl. Stir in the chicken and tuck in the sprig of rosemary.

Warm a heavy-bottomed saucepan over the stove, reduce the heat to medium-high and add the oil. Add the chicken and sauté until sealed all over. Add the wine and stir to loosen the residue from the bottom of the pan. Stir in the stock. Cover the pan, lower the heat, and simmer for 10 to 15 minutes, or until the chicken is cooked through.

Using a draining spoon, remove the chicken from the pan; keep warm. Discard the rosemary. Boil the liquid until reduced by about half. Stir in the cornstarch and return to a boil. Return the chicken to the sauce and stir through. Serve over hot pasta.

Right: Chili Beef with Fresh Cilantro

WILTED SPINACH WITH FAVA BEANS AND PANCETTA

Both beautiful and simple, this dish is reliant on real Italian pancetta, which holds its shape and has good flavor—so you need only a small amount. While the pancetta is cooking, pull the gray skins off the fava beans to reveal the pure jade green within. Serve with narrow, flat pasta, such as tagliolini.

2¹/₂ cups fresh shelled fava beans	2 or 3 garlic cloves, sliced
¹/₂ tablespoon olive oil	11 ounces fresh spinach
7 ounces pancetta, diced	Salt and freshly ground black pepper

Boil the fava beans for a few minutes, depending on size, until just tender, but not soft. Drain, rinse in cold water, and begin peeling off the skins.

Meanwhile, warm a large, heavy-bottomed saucepan over the stove, then add the oil. Add the pancetta and sauté for about 5 minutes. Add the garlic and stir briefly. Add the spinach and stir until just wilted. Add the beans, season to taste with salt and pepper, and stir to mix together. Serve over hot pasta.

DUCK AND HOISIN SAUCE

If you can't resist Peking duck with pancakes, you'll find the flavors you love in this simple sauce. Serve with fine pasta, such as capellini, or with farfalle.

¹/₂ tablespoon peanut oil	1 teaspoon cornstarch, dissolved in
1 or 2 garlic cloves, sliced	2 tablespoons water
2 large duck breasts, about 18 ounces	8 to 10 scallions, cut on the diagonal
in total, skin and fat removed, shredded	¹/₂ cucumber, cut into 2-inch pieces,
6 tablespoons prepared hoisin sauce	finely shredded

Heat the oil in a hot wok or a large skillet. Add the garlic and duck and stir-fry over medium-high heat for 3 to 4 minutes.

Stir the hoisin sauce into the cornstarch. Add to the wok and continue stir-frying for 1 minute, or until thickened. Add a spoonful or two of pasta cooking water if the sauce is too thick.

Serve over hot pasta. Serve the scallions and cucumber in separate bowls for each person to add to his or her pasta.

POTATO AND GARLIC WITH CAVIAR

This recipe uses skim milk to keep the fat content down. Caviar provides a touch of luxury and a color contrast, but you can always use less-expensive lumpfish roe if cost is an issue. Serve with tomato-flavored pasta as a first course.

2¹/₂ cups peeled and diced potatoes	Salt and freshly ground black pepper
2 garlic bulbs, separated into cloves	3 to 4 teaspoons caviar
and peeled	1 bunch fresh chives, snipped
1³/₄ cups skim milk	

Put the potatoes, garlic, and milk in a saucepan and bring to a boil. Lower the heat and simmer for about 15 minutes, or until the potatoes are tender. Strain the milk into a clean saucepan. Push the potatoes and garlic through a strainer or potato ricer into the milk. Season to taste with salt and pepper and reheat gently.

Pour the potato puree over hot pasta, add a spoonful of caviar to each serving, and sprinkle with the chives. Serve at once.

Right: Wilted Spinach with Fava Beans and Pancetta

TUNA PIZZAIOLA

This sauce makes a pantry meal full of great flavors. It looks especially good made with pimento-stuffed Spanish olives. Serve with penne.

1/2 tablespoon olive oil	*1 tablespoon capers, drained*
1 onion, minced	*4 tablespoons halved pitted brine-cured,*
1 to 2 garlic cloves, minced	*Spanish olives, rinsed*
2 cans (14-oz.) crushed tomatoes	*2 cans (7-oz.) tuna in water, drained*
6 canned anchovy fillets, rinsed (see page 7)	*Freshly ground black pepper*
and chopped	*2 tablespoons finely chopped fresh parsley*

Warm a heavy-bottomed saucepan over the stove, then add the oil. Add the onion, cover the pan, and cook over low heat until soft. Add the garlic and tomatoes and simmer for 10 minutes until slightly thicker.

Stir in the anchovies, capers, olives, and tuna and continue simmering for 2 minutes, or until heated through. Season with black pepper. Toss with hot pasta and serve garnished with parsley.

SALMON TERIYAKI

The Japanese wines give a slightly fuller flavor than ordinary sweet wine and sherry to the sauce, which seeps into the pasta and imparts even more flavor as you break into the fish. Serve with tagliatelle.

4 salmon steaks or fillets	*4 tablespoons tamari*
4 tablespoons mirin (sweet rice wine)	*1 garlic clove, cut into fine slivers*
or sweet white wine	*1 teaspoon vegetable oil*
4 tablespoons sake (rice wine) or dry sherry	

Lay the salmon in a shallow dish. Put the mirin, sake, tamari, and garlic into a small saucepan and bring to a boil. Pour over the fish and let marinate for 15 to 20 minutes.

Warm a heavy-bottomed skillet over medium-high heat. Brush the oil over the hot pan, then add the fish and cook for 2 to 3 minutes, brushing with some of the marinade. Using a spatula, carefully turn the fish over and brush again with the marinade. Cook for 1 to 2 minutes longer, or until done to your liking. Serve at once on a bed of hot pasta, spooning over a little more of the marinade if you like.

MUSSELS AND SAFFRON

Mussels are inexpensive, nutritious, and, after you've cleaned them, delightfully quick to cook. Serve with linguine.

4 1/2 pounds mussels, thoroughly cleaned	*Good pinch saffron strands, mixed*
(see page 9)	*with 1 tablespoon hot water*
3/4 cup dry white wine	*1/2 cup low-fat plain yogurt*
2 teaspoons cornstarch, dissolved in	*2 tablespoons finely chopped fresh parsley*
2 tablespoons water	

Discard any cracked or open mussels that do not close when sharply tapped. Bring the wine to a boil in a very large, heavy-bottomed saucepan over high heat. Add the mussels and cover the pan. Cook for 1 to 2 minutes, or until the mussels open; do not overcook them or they will shrink and become tough.

Remove the mussels from the pan using a large draining spoon (you can take them out of their shells if you prefer). Discard any mussels that have remained closed.

Strain the liquid into a measuring cup through a cheesecloth-lined strainer and rinse out the saucepan. Return the liquid to the pan, leaving any grit behind in the measuring cup, and boil until it reduces by half. Stir in the cornstarch and return to a boil. Remove the pan from the heat and stir in the saffron with its water, the yogurt, and the mussels. Heat through very briefly. Serve over hot pasta, garnished with the parsley.

CRAB, LEMON, AND PARSLEY

This Italian-inspired recipe is an easy way to "stretch" a small amount of crab. Serve with linguine or spaghetti.

1 large or 2 small fresh boiled crabs	*Salt and freshly ground black pepper*
(or prepared crabs)	*A few drops anchovy extract or prepared*
4 tablespoons chopped fresh parsley	*Thai fish sauce (optional)*
Grated zest and juice of 1 lemon	*1 tablespoon extra-virgin olive oil*

Remove the meat from the crab and place in a large bowl. Stir in the parsley and most of the lemon zest and juice. Season to taste with salt and pepper and, if you like, add more lemon or a little anchovy extract or fish sauce to bring out the flavor of the crab.

Toss the hot pasta with the olive oil, then with the crab mixture. Serve at once.

Right: Tuna Pizzaiola

VEGETARIAN SAUCES

Almost all vegetables are ideal matches with pasta for quick and easy lunch or supper dishes. The combination of pasta and vegetables also makes good all-in-one side dishes or first courses, as in the traditional Italian menu.

FRESH TOMATO AND BASIL

This must be made with perfect, full-flavored tomatoes, so save this dish for summer cooking, when tomatoes are at their best. Although the sauce is cold, it is traditionally served with very hot spaghetti—use wholewheat spaghetti for a hearty dish.

5½ cups skinned, seeded (see page 9), and diced tomatoes
Salt and freshly ground black pepper
Large handful torn fresh basil leaves, plus extra to serve
1 tablespoon extra-virgin olive oil
1 tablespoon red wine vinegar

Put the tomatoes in a bowl and season well with salt and pepper. Stir in the basil and sprinkle with the oil and vinegar. Cover and leave in the refrigerator for 1 to 2 hours.

To serve, toss hot pasta with the sauce. Serve at once, garnished with extra freshly torn basil leaves.

RICH TOMATO AND OREGANO

With its deep, intense tomato flavor, this is delicious as an accompaniment to broiled fish, chicken, lamb, or pork, as well as hot pasta. The strips of onion and sun-dried tomato cling well to fusilli.

1 tablespoon olive oil
4 large red onions, finely sliced
1 can (14-oz.) crushed tomatoes
1 ounce sun-dried tomatoes (dried, not preserved in oil), cut into thin strips
2 tablespoons chopped fresh oregano
Salt and freshly ground black pepper

Warm a heavy-bottomed saucepan over the stove, then add the oil. Add the onions, cover with a tight-fitting lid, and cook over low heat for about 15 minutes, uncovering and stirring occasionally to prevent sticking. Uncover and cook for 10 minutes longer. Stir in the canned tomatoes and simmer for 5 to 10 minutes.

Add the sun-dried tomatoes and oregano and simmer 5 minutes longer, or until the sun-dried tomatoes are tender. Season to taste with salt and pepper and toss with hot pasta.

ZUCCHINI AND MINT

This makes a pretty lunch or side dish, especially if served with fusilli bucati, the open pasta spirals that look like curls of hair.

4 cups small, tender zucchini, grated into long strands
1 tablespoon salt
1¼ cups shelled fresh or frozen peas
1½ tablespoons olive oil
1 garlic clove, minced
2 tablespoons shredded fresh mint leaves

Put the long zucchini strands into a colander, sprinkle with the salt, and toss lightly. Leave to drain for 30 to 40 minutes. Rinse the zucchini thoroughly and squeeze dry.

Meanwhile, boil the peas until tender; drain and set aside.

Warm a large saucepan or wok over the stove, then add the oil. Add the garlic and zucchini and stir-fry for 2 to 3 minutes. Add the peas, mint, and hot pasta and toss together. Serve at once.

ARTICHOKE WITH SUN-DRIED TOMATO

Canned artichokes can be transformed into this intriguing sauce in a matter of minutes. Serve with conchiglie or cheese-filled ravioli.

2 cans (14-oz.) artichokes, drained
3 to 4 tablespoons prepared pesto
1 tablespoon olive oil
1 garlic clove, minced
2½ cups thinly sliced button mushrooms
Salt and freshly ground black pepper
2 ounces sun-dried tomatoes, soaked in hot water for 10 minutes, drained, and cut into thin strips
Fresh basil leaves for garnish

Put the artichokes in a saucepan, cover with boiling water, and boil for 2 minutes; drain well. Place in a food processor and puree with the pesto.

Rewarm the same saucepan over medium-high heat, then add the oil. Add the garlic, mushrooms, and salt and pepper to taste and sauté for about 3 minutes. Add the artichoke puree and the sun-dried tomatoes and heat through. Serve over hot pasta, garnished with basil.

ASPARAGUS, CHERVIL, AND LEMON

To make a luxurious sauce without cream, you have to work carefully, because yogurt can curdle when heated. This delicate sauce may sound fussy—and it can't be kept hanging around—but it's worth the effort. Penne echo the shape of the asparagus.

2 cups trimmed asparagus, cut into
   1-inch pieces
2 teaspoons cornstarch, dissolved in
   2 tablespoons water
1 cup low-fat plain yogurt

1 teaspoon coarse mustard
Salt and freshly ground black pepper
4 tablespoons dry white wine
Grated zest of 2 lemons
4 tablespoons chopped fresh chervil

Cook the asparagus in a large saucepan of boiling water for 2 to 3 minutes or until tender. Using a draining spoon, transfer to a colander. (Use the same water to cook your pasta.)

While the pasta is cooking, combine the cornstarch with the yogurt, mustard, and salt and pepper to taste.

Reserve ½ cup of the pasta cooking water and mix together with the wine. Boil until reduced by three-quarters. Remove from the heat and stir in the yogurt mixture. Stir over very low heat until the sauce thickens slightly. Add the pasta, asparagus, lemon zest, and chervil and heat through. Serve at once.

Below: Chargrilled Asparagus with Spanish Olives and Basil

ROASTED VEGETABLE

This combination of vegetables makes a change from the usual Mediterranean mixture. The mushrooms shrink when roasted but their flavor is intensified. For best results, choose cremini mushrooms, about 1½ inches in diameter. Serve with penne or rigatoni.

1 tablespoon olive oil
1½ pounds asparagus, woody bases
   trimmed off
2 red bell peppers, cut into strips about
   ¾ inch wide
3 cups zucchini cut into 1-inch pieces

12 ounces mushrooms
4 tablespoons chopped mixed fresh herbs,
   such as parsley, thyme, and basil
Salt and freshly ground black pepper
4 tablespoons dry white wine

Preheat the oven to its highest setting. Brush a heavy roasting pan with the oil and spread the vegetables over the bottom. Sprinkle with half the herbs, some salt and pepper, and half the wine. Roast for about 20 minutes, or until the vegetables are just tender and beginning to char.

Remove the pan from the oven and chop the asparagus into ¾-inch pieces; you can also chop the other vegetables smaller if you like. Place the roasting pan over high heat. Add the remaining wine and stir to deglaze the pan. Add hot pasta and the remaining herbs and stir together. Serve at once.

ARUGULA, GARLIC, AND GOAT CHEESE

Yes, it sounds like a lot of garlic—but everyone knows garlic is good for you. The cheese melts satisfyingly into a little of the pasta water to make a sauce for small pasta shapes, such as orecchiette or conchiglie.

4 whole garlic bulbs
1 tablespoon olive oil
1 tablespoon fresh thyme leaves

¾ to 1 cup crumbled goat cheese
3 ounces arugula
Salt and freshly ground black pepper

Preheat the oven to 425°F. Separate the garlic into cloves, but do not peel them. Put the cloves on a sheet of foil or baking parchment, sprinkle with the oil, and pinch the edges of the foil or parchment together to make a well-sealed package. Bake for about 25 minutes until tender.

Pop the garlic cloves out of the skins, sprinkle with the thyme, and season to taste with salt and pepper.

Toss hot pasta with the cheese and 2 to 3 tablespoons of the pasta cooking water in the saucepan. Add the arugula and garlic and stir over low heat until the cheese melts and the arugula wilts. Serve at once.

ROASTED TOMATO AND GARLIC

Slow roasting intensifies the flavor of the tomatoes and mellows the garlic. This needs no other accompaniment than green or white tagliatelle, but you can sprinkle with grated cheese or black olives if you are not worried about the extra fat they add.

*3 pounds fresh plum tomatoes or
  vine-ripened tomatoes*
1 tablespoon sea salt

8 garlic cloves, unpeeled
1/2 tablespoon olive oil

Preheat the oven to 300°F. Slice the tomatoes in half and place on a baking sheet lined with baking parchment or aluminum foil. Sprinkle with the salt and place in the oven.

After 1 hour, add the garlic cloves to a corner of the baking sheet and sprinkle with the olive oil. Roast for 1 hour longer.

Reserve 12 tomato halves. Peel the roasted garlic and combine with the remaining tomatoes in a blender or food processor. Blend to create a coarse sauce and toss with hot pasta. Serve with the reserved tomatoes on top.

CHARGRILLED ASPARAGUS WITH SPANISH OLIVES AND BASIL

The slightly charred flavor of the asparagus is a good match for the olive mixture. Olives and basil—and even garlic and Parmesan cheese—vary in strength of flavor, so I suggest you begin with the given quantities, but have more on hand and be prepared to adjust according to taste. The olive mixture can be prepared a day ahead, which mellows the flavors. Radiatore pasta is perfect to trap the little bits of olive paste.

*1 1/2 pounds asparagus, woody bases
  trimmed off*
2 teaspoons olive oil
*3/4 cup pitted Spanish olives in brine,
  rinsed and patted dry*

Large handful fresh basil leaves
2 garlic cloves, roughly chopped
3/4 cup shaved low-fat Parmesan cheese
1 tablespoon olive oil (optional)
Freshly ground black pepper

Warm a grill pan or broiler until it is very hot. If your asparagus is really fresh and the stalks are juicy when you snap off the bottom, you can brush them with the olive oil and cook with no further ado. If you are suspicious about its age, I suggest you plunge the asparagus into boiling water for a minute, then drain and grill or broil it.

Put the olives, basil, garlic, Parmesan cheese, and pepper to taste into a food processor and process to a coarse puree, scraping down the side of the bowl after 30 seconds. Taste and add more basil, olives, or Parmesan if you like. You can also add 1 tablespoon of olive oil, if you are not worried about the small amount of extra fat.

Toss the olive mixture with hot pasta. Cut the asparagus into 2-inch lengths and add to the pasta. Serve at once.

Above: *Roasted Tomato and Garlic*

MUSHROOMS WITH TRUFFLE OIL

Don't worry if you can't find truffle oil—even without it the sauce is still intensely mushroom flavored. Linguine offers a good pale contrast to the dark, black liquid.

1 1/2 ounces dried porcini mushrooms, sliced
5 3/4 cups sliced large fresh mushrooms
2 or 3 garlic cloves, sliced

2 tablespoons tamari
Truffle oil

Put the dried mushrooms in a measuring cup and add 7 ounces hot water. Leave to soak for about 30 minutes.

Fish out the mushrooms and squeeze them gently over the cup to collect the liquid. Strain the liquid through a paper-towel-lined strainer into a saucepan. Check the soaked mushrooms for grit, then add them to the saucepan with the fresh mushrooms, garlic, and tamari. Bring to a rapid boil, stirring occasionally, for about 5 minutes until the mushrooms are tender and the liquid reduces to a few tablespoons.

Spoon over hot pasta and sprinkle each serving with a few drops of truffle oil.

LEMON AND PINE NUT WITH THYME GREMOLATA

This is a delicate and pretty sauce that works best with a small amount of pasta (no more than six ounces for four people) as a first course or side dish. Don't skimp on the lemons—they are a key ingredient, so buy unwaxed ones and have an extra one ready in case you want a stronger lemon flavor. Serve with a fine pasta such as tagliolini or capelli d'angelo (angel's hair).

FOR THE THYME GREMOLATA:

Finely shredded zest of 1 unwaxed lemon
1 tablespoon fresh thyme leaves

1/2 garlic clove, minced
Salt and freshly ground black pepper

FOR THE SAUCE:

1 garlic clove, minced
1 tablespoon olive oil
2 tablespoons pine nuts
2 tablespoons lemon juice

Finely shredded zest of 1 unwaxed lemon
4 tablespoons finely chopped fresh parsley
Salt and freshly ground black pepper

Mix together the ingredients for the thyme gremolata; set aside.

Sauté the garlic in the oil over low heat for 2 to 3 minutes. Stir in the remaining ingredients and season to taste. Toss with hot pasta and 2 tablespoons of the pasta cooking water. Serve at once, sprinkled with the thyme gremolata.

TOMATO–MACARONI GRATIN

In a reversal of the usual macaroni and cheese dish, this recipe features macaroni mixed with a tomato sauce and topped with cheese before the whole dish goes in the oven. Use a strongly flavored or sharp cheese and you will need only a small amount. This dish is very filling—allow 11 ounces macaroni for four people.

1/2 tablespoon olive oil
1 onion, minced
2 garlic cloves, minced
2 teaspoon dried oregano
2 cans (14-oz.) crushed tomatoes

Salt and freshly ground black pepper
1 cup fresh wholewheat bread crumbs
1/2 cup grated low-fat Parmesan cheese or
*   sharp low-fat cheddar cheese*

Preheat the oven to 400°F.

Warm a heavy-bottomed saucepan over the stove, then add the oil. Add the onion, cover, and cook until it is soft. Add the garlic and half the oregano and stir to bring out the aromas. Add the tomatoes and simmer for 3 to 4 minutes longer. Season to taste with salt and pepper and mix with cooked macaroni.

Tip the mixture into a baking dish. Mix the bread crumbs with the cheese and remaining oregano and sprinkle over the macaroni. Bake for 10 to 15 minutes, or until the topping is crisp and brown.

SPICY SPINACH AND LENTIL

The inspiration for this dish is Persian. If you really want to go to town, prepare another batch of saffron in hot water and drizzle it over the yogurt just before serving. Serve with tagliatelle.

1/4 cup green lentils
1 bay leaf
Pinch vegetable bouillon granules
9 ounces fresh spinach
1 tablespoon olive oil
1 teaspoon ground coriander
1 teaspoon ground cumin

1 teaspoon peeled, minced fresh ginger
1 garlic clove, minced
Salt and freshly ground black pepper
Good pinch saffron strands, mixed
*   with 1 tablespoon hot water*
2/3 cup plain yogurt
Small bunch fresh cilantro

Put the lentils, bay leaf, bouillon granules, and 2 cups water into a saucepan and bring to a boil. Boil rapidly for 10 minutes, lower the heat, and simmer for about 20 minutes until the lentils are tender and the liquid is absorbed.

Meanwhile, rinse the spinach well and leave to drain.

Warm a large saucepan over the stove, then add the oil. Add the coriander and cumin and sauté for 1 to 2 minutes over low heat. Add the ginger, garlic, and salt and pepper to taste and stir for 30 seconds. Add the spinach and stir until it wilts and is coated in the spices.

Stir the saffron into the lentils, then add to the spinach and stir briefly. Serve on a bed of pasta, topped with the yogurt and fresh cilantro.

Right: Lemon and Pine Nut with Thyme Gremolata

Vegetable Spaghetti

The secret of this bright and colorful dish is to cut the vegetables into very fine strips so they cook quickly and retain their vibrant colors along with as many nutrients as possible. The pine nuts add extra texture and fiber, but can be omitted if you want to keep the overall fat content very low. Although they are very high in fat, only a small amount per serving is used here, and they do not contain any cholesterol. Serve with linguine.

1 tablespoon olive oil	1 young leek, cut into 3-inch pieces and
1 garlic clove, sliced	then into thin strips
5 sprigs fresh thyme	4 tablespoons dry white wine
1/2 cup green beans sliced lengthwise	4 tablespoons vegetable stock
2 young carrots, cut into thin strips	1 to 2 teaspoons balsamic vinegar
1/2 red and 1/2 yellow bell peppers,	Salt and freshly ground black pepper
cut into thin strips	2 tablespoons pine nuts (optional)

Warm a large saucepan or wok over the stove, then add the oil. Add the garlic, thyme, green beans, carrots, peppers, and leeks and stir-fry for 1 to 2 minutes.

Add the wine and stock and continue stir-frying over high heat for 2 to 3 minutes until the liquid reduces to about 2 tablespoons; do not overcook. Add balsamic vinegar and salt and pepper to taste and toss with hot pasta. Sprinkle with the pine nuts and serve at once.

Below: Vegetable Spaghetti

Chargrilled Leek and Red Onion with Salsa Verde

There are many versions of salsa verde, a piquant parsley relish often served with fish. You can use arugula, cilantro, or mint instead of the basil. Casareccie pasta goes well with this.

1 pound thin leeks, trimmed and cleaned	1 teaspoon Dijon mustard
4 red onions	1 tablespoon lemon juice
Large bunch fresh parsley, chopped	2 tablespoons extra-virgin olive oil, plus
Handful fresh basil leaves	a little extra for brushing the grill
1 garlic clove, crushed	Salt and freshly ground black pepper
1 tablespoon capers, drained	Grated lemon zest, to garnish

Blanch the leeks in boiling water for 1 minute, then drain and refresh in cold water. Cut the onions in half down through the root end, then cut each half into 3 wedges, but do not separate the wedges. Blanch in boiling water for 1 to 2 minutes. Drain, refresh in cold water, and leave to drain.

Pound the parsley, basil, garlic, and capers in a mortar until smooth. Add the mustard and lemon juice and stir well. Using a fork, gradually whisk in the olive oil. Season to taste with salt and pepper.

Warm a grill pan or heavy-bottomed skillet over high heat. When it is very hot, brush it with olive oil. Add the leeks and separated onion wedges. Cook for 15 to 20 minutes, turning them over occasionally until they begin to turn black all over.

Toss the salsa verde with hot pasta and serve the vegetables on top. Garnish with lemon zest.

NOTE
Scallions are very good chargrilled, and you don't need to blanch them first; try them instead of leeks.

Fennel and Pecorino

The sharpness of pecorino cheese contrasts well with the sweetness of the fennel; for a mellower flavor, substitute low-fat Parmesan. Serve with conchiglie.

3 or 4 fennel bulbs, about 1 1/2 pounds	1/2 cup grated low-fat pecorino cheese
in total, quartered	Salt and freshly ground black pepper
1 tablespoon olive oil	2 tablespoons snipped fresh chives

Preheat the oven to 450°F. Blanch the fennel in boiling water for 1 to 2 minutes; drain well. Chop the fennel into small pieces and place in a roasting pan with the olive oil. Sprinkle with the cheese, a little salt, and plenty of pepper. Roast for 20 to 30 minutes until the cheese begins to turn golden brown.

Toss with hot pasta and serve garnished with the chives.

MUSHROOM, SPINACH, AND RICOTTA

A vivid green sauce, full of rich flavors. Serve with farfalle.

1 tablespoon olive oil
2 garlic cloves, crushed
3 cups sliced button mushrooms
Salt and freshly ground black pepper

18 ounces fresh spinach, trimmed and
*   washed, or 10 ounces frozen spinach*
Freshly grated nutmeg to taste
¹/₂ cup part-skim ricotta cheese

Warm a large, heavy-bottomed saucepan over the stove, then add the oil. Add the garlic, mushrooms, and salt and pepper to taste and sauté until soft, adding a splash of water if the mushrooms seem too dry. Lift out the mushrooms with a draining spoon; set aside.

Add the spinach to the pan and season with salt, pepper, and nutmeg. Cook until wilted (if fresh) or thawed (if frozen). Put the spinach and any liquid into a food processor or blender. Add the ricotta and puree until smooth.

Return the mushrooms to the pan with the spinach sauce and heat through gently. Toss with hot pasta.

SWEET POTATO AND BROCCOLI

Use golden-fleshed sweet potatoes for this dish: the pale-fleshed sweet potatoes often have a mealy texture. Serve with spirali or rigatoni.

12 ounces sweet potatoes, unpeeled
*   and quartered*
9 ounces broccoli, cut into small florets
1 tablespoon olive oil
1 garlic clove, minced
1 tablespoon peeled, minced fresh ginger
6 scallions, cut diagonally into
*   2-inch pieces*

1 tablespoon soy sauce
1 cup tomato passata (see page 8)
Small handful fresh basil leaves,
*   roughly torn*
Salt and freshly ground black pepper

Boil the sweet potatoes until just tender. Drain, refresh in cold water, and peel. Cut the potatoes into ³/₄-inch chunks. Boil the broccoli until just tender; drain and refresh.

Heat the oil in a hot wok or large, heavy-bottomed skillet. Add the garlic, ginger, and scallions and stir-fry for 30 seconds. Add the broccoli and sweet potatoes and stir-fry for 2 to 3 minutes longer. Add the soy sauce and stir briefly. Stir in the tomato passata and basil and bring to a boil. Season to taste with salt and pepper. Toss with hot pasta and serve at once.

Above: *Roasted Pumpkin and Sage*

ROASTED PUMPKIN AND SAGE

The bright orange cubes of pumpkin are set against a background of tomatoes, sage, and onion that is picked up by the pasta. This is good with spaghetti or casareccie.

1¹/₂ pounds pumpkin or butternut squash,
*   peeled, seeded, and cut into ¹/₂-inch*
*   chunks*
1 onion, chopped
4 tomatoes, skinned, seeded (see page 9),
*   and diced*

Bunch fresh sage leaves or sprigs
1 tablespoon olive oil
4 tablespoons dry white wine
Salt and freshly ground black pepper

Preheat the oven to 450°F. Spread the pumpkin, onion, and tomatoes out in a heavy roasting pan and tuck 4 to 6 large sage leaves or sprigs among them. Drizzle with the olive oil and roast for about 20 minutes until the pumpkin is tender. Meanwhile, finely chop some more sage leaves; you will need about 1 tablespoon.

Remove the roasting pan from the oven. Add the wine and chopped sage and place over medium heat for about 1 minute, stirring to deglaze the pan. Season to taste with salt and pepper. Remove from the heat, add hot pasta, and stir briefly to coat it in the sauce. Serve at once.

HOT & SPICY SAUCES

Pasta provides a perfect background for hot chili- or ginger-based sauces—think of all the classic Asian dishes served with noodles. Some varieties of chili peppers are very hot, while others are mild, and unless you are a chili fanatic it can be difficult to judge the right quantity. I suggest you begin with a small amount, then taste and add more "heat" if you want.

BROCCOLI AND HOT RED PEPPER

Inspired by the Spanish romesco sauce, this version is lighter than the original, which includes large quantities of olive oil and fried bread. You can reduce the fat content even more by not using the almonds, although I suggest only a very small amount divided between four portions. Serve with almost any pasta shape.

3 red bell peppers	Salt and freshly ground black pepper
3 tomatoes	3 cups broccoli florets
2 garlic cloves, roughly chopped	1 tablespoon slivered almonds, lightly
1 to 2 dashes hot pepper sauce	toasted (optional)

Preheat the oven to its highest setting. Put the peppers on a cookie sheet and roast for 15 minutes, or until partly charred. Turn the peppers over, add the tomatoes to the cookie sheet, and roast for 15 minutes longer. Skin the peppers and the tomatoes (see page 9). Puree the peppers and tomatoes (and any juices) with the garlic in a blender or food processor. Season to taste with hot pepper sauce and salt and pepper.

Steam or boil the broccoli; drain well. Arrange it on a bed of hot pasta and pour the sauce over the top. Sprinkle with the almonds, if you like, and serve at once.

BLACK BEAN AND TOMATO

This fusion of Chinese flavorings with tomatoes is great with fusilli, especially the bright-yellow corn fusilli sold in some supermarkets. Look for preserved black beans in Chinese markets.

3 tablespoons salted and fermented Chinese black beans	1-inch piece fresh ginger, peeled
	1 tablespoon olive oil
2 tablespoons rice wine, dry sherry, or vermouth	Generous 1 cup canned whole corn kernels, well drained
2 large garlic cloves	2 cans (14-oz.) crushed tomatoes
1 bunch scallions	2 tablespoons soy sauce

Soak the black beans in the rice wine, sherry, or vermouth while you finely chop the garlic, scallions, and ginger (about 1½ tablespoons).

Warm a large saucepan or wok over the stove, then add the oil. Add the garlic, ginger, and half the scallions and stir-fry for 1 minute. Add the black beans and corn kernels and stir for a few seconds. Add the tomatoes and soy sauce and heat through. Serve on hot pasta, sprinkled with the remaining scallions.

ROASTED CORN AND ZUCCHINI SALSA

This bright and colorful vegetarian sauce is best served with pasta shells to trap the corn kernels. Invest in a fresh pack of ground cumin—the brown dust that's been in your pantry for months will do nothing for this dish.

2 corn cobs	2 tablespoons finely chopped fresh cilantro
3 cups zucchini cut into 2-inch chunks	1 tablespoon fresh lime juice
1 tablespoon olive oil	4 ripe tomatoes, skinned, seeded
1 tablespoon ground cumin	(see page 9), and diced
Salt and freshly ground black pepper	4 scallions, thinly sliced
1 fresh red chili, minced	

Preheat the oven to 400°F. Place the corn cobs and zucchini chunks on a cookie sheet, brush lightly with the oil, and sprinkle with the cumin and salt and pepper to taste. Roast, turning occasionally, until tender and beginning to brown, 25 to 30 minutes. Leave until cool enough to handle.

Cut the zucchini chunks so that you have half-moon shaped pieces. Hold the corn cobs upright on a chopping board and, using a sharp knife, scrape off the kernels.

Mix the corn and zucchini with the chili, cilantro, lime juice, and tomatoes. Season to taste with salt and pepper and serve on hot pasta, garnished with the scallions.

FIVE-SPICE LAMB

A simple Chinese-style dish that goes well with penne or Chinese egg noodles.

2 teaspoons cornstarch, dissolved in
    2 tablespoons water
1 tablespoon dry sherry
2 tablespoons soy sauce
1 teaspoon Chinese five-spice powder
1 teaspoon sugar or honey
1 pound lean, boned lamb,
    cut into thin strips

1 tablespoon peanut oil
1 garlic cloves, minced
2 tablespoons peeled, minced fresh ginger
1 fresh red chili, minced
2 bunches scallions, sliced on the
    diagonal into 2-inch pieces
2 bell peppers (red, green, or yellow)
    sliced thinly into strips

Mix the cornstarch with the sherry, soy sauce, five-spice powder, and sugar or honey. Stir in the lamb and let marinate while you prepare the remaining ingredients.

Heat the oil in a hot wok over high heat. Add the garlic, ginger, and chili and stir-fry for 1 minute. Add the lamb and its marinade and stir-fry for 2 to 3 minutes until the lamb is brown. Add the scallions and bell peppers and stir-fry for 2 to 3 minutes, adding a little water if necessary to prevent sticking. Serve at once over hot pasta.

Below: *Pearl Onion Curry*

PEARL ONION CURRY

Use the smallest onions you can find—or use shallots, which often divide themselves in half when you peel them. Tagliatelle or pappardelle provide the best calm background to the hot, busy sauce.

4 tablespoons golden raisins
1 cup sweet white wine, such as
    a Bordeaux from Loupiac or
    Monbazillac
20 to 24 pearl onions or shallots (about
    2½ cups), unpeeled
1½ cups carrot cut into matchsticks
1¾ cups thinly sliced leeks

2 tablespoons mild curry paste
Large pinch turmeric
1 cup vegetable stock
1 tablespoon liquid from mango chutney
4 tablespoons plain yogurt
1 dessert apple, peeled, cored, and diced
Salt and freshly ground black pepper
2 tablespoons roughly chopped fresh cilantro

Soak the raisins in 2 tablespoons of the wine; set aside.

Meanwhile, blanch the onions or shallots in boiling water for 1 to 2 minutes. Drain and refresh in cold water, then peel and place in a small, heavy-bottomed saucepan (just large enough to hold them in a single layer) with the remaining wine. Cover the pan, place over low heat, and simmer slowly, shaking the pan occasionally, until the onions are tender when pierced with a skewer. Uncover and turn the heat up to medium-high so the wine evaporates and the onions become golden brown.

While the onions are browning, blanch the carrots in boiling water for 1 minute. Drain and refresh; set aside.

Put the leeks, curry paste, turmeric, and stock in a saucepan, cover, and simmer for 8 to 10 minutes until the leeks are tender. Puree in a food processor until smooth. Add the mango chutney liquid and yogurt and puree again. Return to a clean saucepan.

Stir in the apple, the raisins and their soaking liquid, and the blanched carrots and heat through. Season to taste with salt and pepper and serve over hot pasta, topped with the glazed onions and cilantro.

ANCHOVY AND BROCCOLI

In the traditional version of this dish from Apulia in southern Italy, the anchovies are blended into a rich, oily sauce. Here, using very little oil, they still make a delicious sauce for the broccoli and orecchiette or pasta shells.

3 cups broccoli cut into small florets
with the stems sliced into thin "coins"
1 tablespoon olive oil
2 garlic cloves, sliced

1 can (2-oz.) anchovy fillets, rinsed
(see page 7) and chopped
1/2 fresh red chili, minced
Freshly ground black pepper
A few drops chili oil (optional)

Cook the broccoli in boiling water for 2 to 3 minutes; drain and set aside.

Heat the oil in a saucepan over low heat. Add the garlic and anchovies and cook for 2 to 3 minutes, mashing the anchovies so they form a paste. Add the chili and 4 tablespoons of the pasta cooking water and stir well. Add the broccoli and plenty of black pepper.

Toss with hot pasta and mix well. If you like, finish by sprinkling with a few drops of chili oil.

MUSSELS MASALA

Mussels have a strong flavor so they are more than a match for a curry sauce. Try this with tagliatelle.

1 tablespoon peanut oil
1 onion, minced
1 garlic clove, crushed
2 tablespoons curry paste

4 1/2 pounds mussels, thoroughly cleaned
(see page 9)
4 tablespoons plain yogurt
2 tablespoons finely chopped fresh cilantro

Warm a very large, heavy-bottomed saucepan over the stove, then add the oil. Add the onion and garlic and cook until softened. Add the curry paste and cook for 1 minute. Discard any cracked or open mussels that do not close when tapped and add the remainder to the pan. Turn up the heat, cover, and cook for 1 to 2 minutes, or until the mussels open; do not overcook or they will shrink and become tough.

Take the mussels out of the pan with a large draining spoon and remove them from their shells; discard any that have not opened.

Meanwhile, return the pan to the heat and stir in the yogurt. Boil until reduced and thick; the yogurt will curdle, but it doesn't matter in this sauce. Remove from the heat and return the mussels to the sauce. Serve on hot pasta, sprinkled with cilantro.

Above: Anchovy and Broccoli

DUCK AND MANGO

The flavors here are not so much hot as bright and lively, with ginger and lime. Serve with penne.

1/2 tablespoon peanut oil
2 large duck breast halves, about
18 ounces in total, skin and fat removed
and the meat cut into thin strips
2 tablespoons finely shredded fresh ginger
1 tablespoon honey
Finely grated zest of 2 limes

2 tablespoons lime juice
1 mango, peeled, pitted, and cut into
matchsticks
10 to 12 scallions, finely sliced on the
diagonal
Salt and freshly ground black pepper

Warm a large saucepan or a wok over high heat. Add the oil and duck meat and stir-fry for 3 to 4 minutes. Add all the remaining ingredients and stir-fry for 1 to 3 minutes longer until heated through. Season to taste with salt and pepper and toss with hot pasta.

Spicy Moroccan Eggplant

The spices in this vegetarian sauce are mild. Serve with rigatoni or spirali.

1 eggplant, cut into 1/2-inch cubes
Salt and freshly ground black pepper
2 tablespoons vegetable oil
1 onion, minced
2 teaspoons paprika
1/2 teaspoon ground cumin
1/4 teaspoon ground allspice
1/4 teaspoon ground cinnamon
2 garlic cloves, minced

Pinch sugar
Large pinch saffron threads, mixed with
  1 tablespoon hot water
1 small red bell peppper and 1 small yellow
  bell pepper, cut into 3/4-inch dice
2 to 3 tablespoons lemon juice
4 to 6 tablespoons orange juice
2 tablespoons roughly torn fresh basil leaves

Put the eggplant cubes in a colander and sprinkle with plenty of salt; set aside for 20 to 30 minutes. Rinse the eggplant well and return to the colander or place in a steamer. Cover and steam over boiling water for 15 to 20 minutes until tender, stirring once.

Meanwhile, warm a heavy-bottomed saucepan over the stove, then add the oil. Add the onion and spices and cook over medium heat, stirring constantly, for about 2 minutes until fragrant. Add the garlic, sugar, about 1 cup water, and salt and pepper to taste. Cover and simmer gently for 20 minutes, stirring occasionally.

Add the steamed eggplant, the saffron in its water, the bell peppers, 2 tablespoons lemon juice, and 4 tablespoons orange juice. Simmer, uncovered, for 5 to 8 minutes. Taste and add more sugar, lemon juice, orange juice, and salt or pepper as necessary. Stir in the basil. Serve over hot pasta.

Tomato-Curry Sauce with Smoked Tofu

This is a vegetarian recipe, but you can replace the smoked tofu with shelled shrimp or mussels. Serve with fusilli or another pasta with curves to hold the sauce.

1 tablespoon peanut oil
2 teaspoons black mustard seeds
1 leek, finely sliced
4 tomatoes, skinned (see page 9) and
  chopped
1 red bell pepper, roughly chopped

1 teaspoon curry powder
2 tablespoons basmati rice
3/4 cup milk
3/4 cup water
Salt and freshly ground black pepper
7 ounces smoked firm tofu, cubed

Warm a heavy-bottomed saucepan over the stove, then add the oil. Add the mustard seeds and then as soon as they begin to crackle, add the leek. Stir the leek in the oil for 2 minutes. Add all the remaining ingredients, except the tofu, and bring to a boil. Lower the heat and simmer for 20 minutes, or until the rice is very tender.

Puree in a blender or food processor until smooth; season to taste with salt and pepper. Return the sauce to a clean saucepan, add the tofu, and simmer for 5 minutes until heated through. Serve over hot pasta.

Right: Spicy Moroccan Eggplant

HOT SHRIMP WITH BASIL

Simple, delicious, and versatile, this can be made with cooked or raw shrimp, fresh or dried chili, or hot pepper sauce, and just about any type of pasta.

2-inch piece fresh ginger, peeled and
    roughly chopped
2 garlic cloves, chopped
1 teaspoon salt
1 teaspoon sugar
2 teaspoons vinegar

1 tablespoon vegetable oil
11 ounces shrimp (see headnote)
1 small red chili, finely sliced, or
    1 to 2 dashes hot pepper sauce
4 tablespoons shredded fresh basil leaves

Using a mortar and pestle, or a spice grinder, blend together the ginger, garlic, salt, sugar, vinegar, and oil. Heat a skillet or wok over low heat. Add the spice paste and stir-fry for about 2 minutes, stirring occasionally.

Add the shrimp, chili or hot pepper sauce, and shredded basil and cook for 2 to 3 minutes longer until the shrimp are cooked or heated through. Serve over hot pasta.

Below: Hot Shrimp with Basil

CRAB, GINGER, AND BABY CORN

Salty, sweet, and citrus flavors come together in this colorful dish inspired by traditional Thai salads. I have kept the flavors fairly mild, but let your tastebuds tell you whether to add more ginger, chili, lemongrass, or lime. Tagliatelle is my preferred pasta for this sauce.

1 tablespoon peanut oil
2 tablespoons peeled, minced fresh ginger
2 garlic cloves, minced
1 fresh red chili, minced
2 lemongrass stalks, peeled and minced
1½ cups drained baby corn, sliced
    diagonally if large

2 cups snow peas sliced diagonally
Fresh crabmeat from 2 crabs
    (about 10 ounces total)
2 tablespoons soy sauce
Juice of ½ to 1 lime
2 tablespoons chopped fresh cilantro

Warm a wok or large saucepan over the stove, then add the oil. Add the ginger, garlic, chili, and lemongrass and stir-fry for 1 minute. Add the baby corn and snow peas and stir-fry for 2 to 3 minutes. Add the crabmeat, soy sauce, and lime juice and toss over high heat for about 1 minute.

Stir in the hot pasta. Serve at once, topped with the cilantro.

SQUID WITH LEMONGRASS

This Thai-style dish is good served with fine vermicelli noodles or tagliatelle.

1 whole squid, about 1¼ pounds, or
    1 pound dressed squid
Juice of 1½ limes
2 tablespoons prepared Thai fish sauce
1 tablespoon soy sauce
2 garlic cloves, crushed

2 teaspoons light brown sugar
1 large lemongrass stalk, peeled and
    minced
1 small dried chili, crushed
1 tablespoon peanut oil
Handful fresh cilantro, finely chopped

Prepare the squid if using whole squid (see page 9). Score the bodies lightly on both sides and cut into 1-inch squares. Mix together all the remaining ingredients, except the oil and cilantro, in a nonmetallic bowl. Add the squid and let marinate for 20 to 30 minutes.

Warm a wok or a large saucepan over high heat. When it is very hot, add the oil and the squid with its marinade and stir-fry for about 1 minute until the squid is just cooked through. Serve at once on hot pasta, sprinkled with the cilantro.

CHICKEN CHILI WITH CHICKPEAS

Tomatoes, ginger, and cumin go together surprisingly well. Chickpeas may sound an unnecessarily heavy addition to a pasta dish, but there are several precedents in traditional Italian cooking, and they add bulk and flavor without fat. Serve with macaroni.

1 tablespoon peanut oil	2 teaspoons ground cumin
2¹/₂ cups cubed, skinless chicken breast meat	¹/₂ teaspoon cayenne pepper
	1 can (14-oz.) crushed tomatoes
3 garlic cloves, crushed	1 cup canned chickpeas, drained
2 tablespoons minced, peeled fresh ginger	Salt and freshly ground black pepper

Warm a heavy-bottomed saucepan over the stove; reduce the heat to medium-high and add the oil. Add the chicken and quickly seal all over. Remove the chicken with a draining spoon; set aside.

Add the garlic, ginger, cumin, cayenne, and 1 to 2 spoonfuls water to the pan, stirring to loosen the chicken residue from the bottom. Add the tomatoes and cook until they just begin to simmer. Return the chicken to the pan, cover, and simmer for 10 to 15 minutes.

Add the chickpeas and simmer for 5 minutes. Season to taste and serve over hot pasta.

PORK, PINEAPPLE, AND CILANTRO

This is an easy dish with lively, fruity flavors. Serve with a thin, delicate pasta, such as tagliolini or vermicelli.

14 ounces lean ground pork	¹/₂ cup tomato passata (see page 8)
1 onion, minced	1¹/₄ cups canned pineapple chunks in natural juice, or fresh pineapple chunks
1 garlic clove, crushed	
1 tablespoon minced, peeled fresh ginger	Juice of ¹/₂ lime
1 or 2 fresh red chilies, cut into thin rings	4 tablespoons chopped fresh cilantro
2 tablespoons soy sauce, plus more if needed	Salt and freshly ground black pepper

Warm a saucepan over the stove; reduce the heat to medium-high and add the pork and onion. Cover and cook for 5 to 7 minutes, stirring occasionally to break up the meat. Add the garlic, ginger, chili, soy sauce, and passata, cover, and simmer over low heat for 20 to 25 minutes.

Stir in the pineapple and heat through for 2 to 3 minutes. Add the lime juice and cilantro, plus more soy sauce or salt and pepper to taste. Serve over hot pasta.

Above: Clams with White Wine, Garlic, and Chili

CLAMS WITH WHITE WINE, GARLIC, AND CHILI

Make this classic dish milder or hotter by using less or more chili. Serve with spaghetti.

2¹/₄ pounds clams in their shells	1 or 2 fresh red chilies, minced
²/₃ cup dry white wine	4 tablespoons finely chopped fresh parsley
1 tablespoon olive oil	Freshly ground black pepper
2 garlic cloves, minced	

Soak the clams in cold water for 1 hour, then wash them well. Discard any clams with cracked shells or ones that do not close when tapped firmly.

Bring the wine to a boil in a saucepan. Add the clams, cover the pan, and boil until the shells open, about 2 minutes; you may need to do this in 2 batches. Discard any clams that do not open.

Using a draining spoon, transfer the clams to a colander. Boil the liquid in the pan until reduced by half. Pour through a cheesecloth-lined strainer into a measuring cup, leaving behind any grit.

Place the olive oil, garlic, chili, and parsley in a clean saucepan. As soon as they start to sizzle and become fragrant, add the clams, the strained cooking liquid, and hot spaghetti. Season with black pepper and stir gently to mix well. Serve at once.

SUBSTANTIAL SAUCES

When pasta takes center stage, it's easy to upgrade it to luxury class. As the following low-fat recipes illustrate,

you don't need to add cream to make a pasta dish that's fit for any feast.

SALMON WITH SOY, MUSTARD, AND DILL

If you're a fan of gravlax, this is the sauce for you. Look for a chum salmon fillet, because it is one of the least fatty salmons. Although a fatty fish, salmon contains Omega-3 oils, believed to be beneficial for your heart. Serve on fresh tagliatelle.

2½ tablespoons cider vinegar	Salt and freshly ground black pepper
3 tablespoons coarse mustard	1 pound salmon fillet, skinned
2 tablespoons light brown sugar	2 tablespoons tamari
2 tablespoons vegetable oil	3 to 4 tablespoons chopped fresh dill

Mix together the vinegar, mustard, and sugar. Whisk in the oil and season to taste with salt and pepper.

Cut the salmon into strips 1 inch wide. Toss with the tamari and 1 tablespoon of the mustard mixture. Stir-fry in a hot wok or heavy-bottomed skillet for 1 to 2 minutes; do not overcook or the salmon will break up.

Add the dill to the remaining mustard mixture. Toss with the salmon, and serve at once on a bed of hot pasta.

WHITE BEAN AND ROSEMARY WITH TRUFFLE OIL

Truffle oil is worth the extravagance—it lasts for ages and it really does elevate the humble bean to great heights. Serve with farfalle.

1 can (14-oz.) cannellini or haricot beans, drained and rinsed	1 to 2 teaspoons truffle oil
1¼ cups well-flavored vegetable stock	Salt and freshly ground black pepper
2 sprigs fresh rosemary	1 tablespoon snipped fresh chives

Put the beans in a saucepan with the stock and rosemary. Cover and simmer for 10 minutes.

Remove the rosemary. In a blender or food processor, puree the stock with about two-thirds of the beans and 1 teaspoon of the truffle oil. Return to the saucepan and heat through. Season to taste with salt and pepper and pour over hot pasta. Sprinkle a few drops of truffle oil, some freshly ground black pepper, and the chives over the pasta. Serve at once.

MUSSELS, FENNEL, AND PERNOD

The combination of mussels and fennel is delicious, and a splash of an aniseed-flavored spirit accentuates both ingredients. Serve with orecchiette or conchiglie.

1 tablespoon olive oil	4½ pounds mussels, cleaned (see page 9)
2 fennel bulbs, finely chopped	2 tablespoons chopped fresh parsley
1 garlic clove, crushed	1 tablespoon chopped fresh dill
½ lemon	
1 tablespoon Pernod or other aniseed-flavored liquor	

Warm a large, heavy-bottomed saucepan over the stove, then add the oil. Add the fennel and garlic and cook over low heat until soft. Add a squeeze of lemon juice, the aniseed-flavored liquor, and the mussels. Turn up the heat, cover the pan, and cook for 1 to 2 minutes, or until the mussels open; do not overcook them or they will shrink and become tough. Discard any mussels that do not open.

Serve over hot pasta, garnished with the parsley and dill.

CAJUN CHICKEN

You should have most of the ingredients for this spicy dish in your pantry—the technique is just a matter of leaving the chicken to absorb the flavors. You can also use turkey. Serve with spirali.

1½ teaspoons paprika	1 tablespoon olive oil, plus more if needed
1½ teaspoons dried oregano	1 onion, chopped
1 teaspoon dried thyme	3 celery ribs, chopped
1 teaspoon cayenne pepper	1 large green bell pepper, chopped
1½ teaspoons salt	2 garlic cloves, chopped
1½ teaspoons black pepper	½ cup beer
3½ cups skinless chicken breast meat cut into bite-size chunks	1½ cups canned crushed tomatoes

Mix together the paprika, oregano, thyme, cayenne, and salt and pepper. Rub into the chicken and leave for at least 2 hours.

Warm a heavy-bottomed saucepan over the stove, then add the oil. Add the chicken and cook until sealed all over. Remove the chicken from the pan. Add the onion, celery, green pepper, and garlic and cook, stirring often, until tender; add another ½ tablespoon oil if necessary to prevent sticking. Return the chicken to the pan and stir in the beer. Cover and simmer for 15 to 20 minutes until the chicken is cooked through and any juices run clear when the chunks are pierced.

Stir in the tomatoes and heat through. Serve over hot pasta.

MIXED SEAFOOD

If you don't like mussels or squid, substitute clams, shelled shrimp, or pieces of a firm fish such as monkfish. Just remember not to overcook any fish or shellfish or it will become tough. Spaghetti, spaghettini, or linguine are traditional for this dish.

1 pound squid, dressed (see page 9)	5 cups skinned, seeded (see page 9), and
2 pounds mussels in their shells,	chopped tomatoes
cleaned (see page 9)	8 jumbo shrimp
1 tablespoon olive oil	2 tablespoons finely chopped fresh parsley
1 garlic clove, sliced	

Slit one side of each squid body and score the inner side with parallel lines 1/2 inch apart, then score in a diagonal direction to make a lattice pattern; if the squid are very small you can leave them whole, otherwise cut them into chunks. Keep the tentacles in bunches, but trim off any hard parts.

Discard any mussels with cracked shells or mussels that do not close when tapped. Put the mussels into a large, wide saucepan. Cover with a tight-fitting lid and place over high heat for 1 to 2 minutes, or until the mussels open; discard any mussels that do not open. Remove and discard most of the shells. Keep the mussels in a covered bowl. Strain the liquid, leaving any grit behind; set the liquid aside.

Warm a large saucepan over the stove, then add the oil. Add the garlic and tomatoes and simmer for 15 to 20 minutes until thicker. Add the squid, shrimp, and 4 tablespoons of the mussel cooking liquid and simmer for 3 to 4 minutes until the squid is just cooked. Add the mussels and heat through briefly. Serve at once over hot pasta, garnished with the parsley.

LIVER VENEZIANA

A satisfying, all-in-one variation on the classic. Serve with fettuccine.

2 tablespoons olive oil	Salt and freshly ground black pepper
5 cups thinly sliced onions	1 tablespoon balsamic vinegar
1 1/4 pounds calf's liver, thinly sliced	2 tablespoons finely chopped fresh parsley

Warm a heavy-bottomed skillet over the stove; reduce the heat to low and add 1 tablespoon of oil. Add the onions, stir to coat in the oil, and cover the pan tightly so they cook in their own steam for 20 to 25 minutes. Stir occasionally.

Meanwhile, trim any membrane and tubes from the liver. Cut the liver into 1-inch squares.

Turn up the heat under the onions and season generously with salt and pepper. Push the onions to the side of the pan. Add the remaining oil and the liver and cook, stirring frequently, for 1 to 2 minutes; the liver should remain pink and juicy inside. As soon as the liver is cooked, sprinkle in the balsamic vinegar and adjust the seasoning. Serve at once over hot pasta, garnished with the parsley.

LENTIL AND SHIITAKE

Although vegetarian, this is a "meaty" sauce. The lentil mixture can be prepared in advance. Serve with tagliatelle.

Generous 1/2 cup green or brown lentils	Salt and freshly ground black pepper
1 bay leaf	1 tablespoon olive oil
1 onion, minced	1 garlic clove, crushed
1 carrot, cut into 1/2-inch dice	1 3/4 cups sliced shiitake mushrooms
1 celery rib, minced	2 tablespoons grated low-fat Parmesan
2 tablespoons tamari	cheese

Rinse the lentils thoroughly. Put them in a saucepan with 3 cups water, the bay leaf, onion, carrot, and celery. Bring to a boil. Lower the heat and simmer for 20 to 30 minutes until the lentils are soft. Mash the mixture lightly and season to taste with tamari and salt and pepper.

Warm a skillet over the stove, then add the oil. Add the garlic and mushrooms and sauté for 2 to 3 minutes. Season to taste with salt and pepper and stir into the lentil mixture. Serve over hot pasta, garnished with the cheese.

PASTA CON LE SARDE

There are many interpretations of this unusual Sicilian dish. In some, the sardines are deep-fried, but here, to keep the fat content down, they are baked. Some recipes use spaghetti but it is very difficult to eat with this sauce, so I suggest penne.

12 fresh sardines, dressed	1 onion, chopped
1/2 cup dried currants	1/2 cup pine nuts
1 fennel bulb, quartered	Salt and freshly ground black pepper
1 tablespoon olive oil	

Preheat the oven to 400°F. Cut the heads and fins off the sardines and cut open the belly from head to tail. Open out the flaps, backbone upward, and press along the spine of the fish to loosen the bone. Turn the fish over and pull out the backbone. (Alternatively, ask your fish merchant to do this.)

Meanwhile, soak the currants in warm water for 10 minutes. Drain and pat dry; set aside. Blanch the fennel in boiling water for 2 minutes. Drain well and chop.

Warm a heavy-bottomed saucepan over the stove, then add the oil. Add the onion and cook until soft and golden. Add the fennel and cook for 5 minutes. Stir in the currants and pine nuts and cook for 2 to 3 minutes longer. Season to taste with salt and pepper.

Toss the hot pasta with the fennel mixture and place in a baking dish. Arrange the sardines on top, cover, and bake for 15 to 20 minutes. Serve at once.

Right: Mixed Seafood

PUMPKIN WITH DATES, CHICKPEAS, AND SAFFRON

The timing of this dish will vary with the type and age of the pumpkin; don't add the dates until the pumpkin is almost tender, because you want them to hold their shapes. Use a pasta that will take up some of the sauce, such as radiatore or gnocchetti sardi.

1 tablespoon olive oil	Good pinch saffron threads
1 onion, thinly sliced	1 small pumpkin, about 1¹/₂ pounds, peeled
1 teaspoon ground ginger	seeds removed, and cut into 1-inch chunks
1 teaspoon ground cinnamon	1 can (14-oz.) chickpeas, drained
1 teaspoon ground cumin	3¹/₂ ounces dates, halved lengthwise and
1 teaspoon paprika	pits removed
Salt and freshly ground black pepper	2 tablespoons chopped fresh parsley
1¹/₂ cups vegetable stock	

Warm a large saucepan over the stove, then add the oil. Add the onion, cover with a tight-fitting lid, and cook until soft, about 10 minutes. Stir in the spices and salt and pepper to taste and cook for 2 minutes longer, stirring frequently. Add the stock and saffron, cover, and simmer over low heat for about 20 minutes.

Add the pumpkin. Simmer, uncovered, for 6 to 8 minutes, until the pumpkin is almost tender. Stir in the chickpeas and dates and simmer for 3 minutes longer. Serve over hot pasta, garnished with parsley.

ROASTED ROOTS WITH LASSI

An earthy vegetarian dish for a winter evening. The vegetables are moistened with a mildly spiced yogurt sauce—if you are in any doubt about the freshness of your cumin, don't use it. Serve with pasta shells or penne.

3 cups carrots, cut into large chunks	8 ounces vacuum-packed or canned
3 cups celery root, cut into large chunks	chestnuts, well drained
2 tablespoons olive oil	Salt and freshly ground black pepper
1 tablespoon soy sauce or tamari	1 cup plain yogurt
1 red onion, cut into 8 wedges	¹/₂ teaspoon ground cumin
3 cups button mushrooms	2 garlic cloves, crushed

Preheat the oven to 400°F. Place a heavy roasting pan in the oven to warm.

Parboil the carrots and celery root separately for about 1 minute; drain well.

Mix the olive oil and soy sauce or tamari in a large bowl. Add the carrots, celery root, onion, mushrooms, and chestnuts and toss to coat. Season generously with salt and pepper. Place into the hot roasting pan and roast for 30 to 40 minutes, or until tender.

Mix the yogurt with the cumin, garlic, and salt and pepper to taste. Toss the vegetables with hot pasta and spoon the yogurt mixture over the top. Serve at once.

PAPRIKA PORK

Pork shoulder, trimmed of all excess fat, gives a meltingly tender result. Serve with tagliatelle.

1 tablespoon peanut oil	2 teaspoons paprika, plus extra for dusting
2 onions, chopped	Salt
1 pound boneless, lean pork, cubed	1 cup plain yogurt
2 tomatoes, skinned, seeded (see page 9),	1 tablespoon poppy seeds
and chopped	

Warm a heavy-bottomed saucepan over the stove; reduce the heat to low and add the oil. Add the onions and cook until soft and golden. Move them to the side of the pan and add the pork. Cook, stirring often, for 5 to 8 minutes.

Stir in the tomatoes, paprika, and a good pinch of salt. Add ¹/₂ cup water and bring to a boil. Cover with a tight-fitting lid, lower the heat, and simmer for about 50 minutes. Add a little more water from time to time to keep the mixture moist.

When the pork is tender and cooked through, remove from the heat, and stir in two-thirds of the yogurt. Serve on hot pasta tossed with the poppy seeds. Top with the remaining yogurt dusted with paprika.

SAFFRON CHICKEN AND SHRIMP

Chicken, shellfish, and saffron are a happy partnership. You can use cooked or uncooked shrimp, in or out of their shells. Serve with spirali or casareccie.

1 tablespoon olive oil	Pinch paprika
3 cups skinned chicken meat,	1 cup peas or chopped green beans
cut into chunks	4 tomatoes, skinned, seeded (see page 9),
1 onion, chopped	and chopped
1 large red bell pepper, cut into strips	8 to 12 large shrimp (see headnote)
2 garlic cloves, chopped	2 tablespoons chopped fresh parsley
Good pinch saffron strands, soaked in	Salt and freshly ground black pepper
a little warm water	¹/₂ lemon

Warm a deep, heavy-bottomed skillet over the stove, then add the oil. Add the chicken and quickly seal all over. Remove with a draining spoon; set aside. Add the onion, pepper, and garlic to the pan and cook until the onion is soft and golden. Stir in the chicken, saffron and its liquid, and paprika, cover with a tight-fitting lid, and cook over low heat for 10 to 15 minutes until the chicken is tender; add a splash of water if necessary to prevent sticking.

Meanwhile, cook the peas or beans in boiling water until just tender. Drain and refresh in cold water; set aside.

When the chicken is cooked through, stir in the peas or beans, tomatoes, shrimp, and parsley. Season generously with salt and pepper and squeeze in some lemon juice to heighten the flavor. Heat through for 2 to 3 minutes longer. Toss with hot pasta and serve at once.

Right: Pumpkin with Dates, Chickpeas, and Saffron

Artichokes, Peas, and Prosciutto

If you can find them, use 1 pound of quartered baby artichokes, instead of the artichoke bottoms. This sauce is very good with casareccie.

2 small hearts of lettuce, shredded	*4 tablespoons vegetable stock or water*
1½ cups fresh shelled or frozen peas	*Salt and freshly ground black pepper*
2 small young carrots, diced	*½ lemon*
8 scallions, chopped	*4 artichoke bottoms (see page 9), trimmed*
2 tablespoons chopped fresh parsley	*4 ounces lean prosciutto, cut into thin strips*

Put the lettuce into a heavy-bottomed saucepan. Add the peas, carrots, scallions, parsley, stock or water, and salt and pepper to taste. Cover with a tight-fitting lid and simmer over very low heat for about 15 minutes until the peas and carrots are tender.

Meanwhile, bring a saucepan of water to a boil with the juice of the lemon and the squeezed remains. Add the artichokes and boil for 10 to 15 minutes, or until tender. Drain and rinse in cold water; slice. Add the artichokes and prosciutto to the pea mixture and heat through for about 2 minutes. Serve tossed with hot pasta.

Red Mullet with Fennel and Orange

Don't worry if you can't get red mullet—pale, firm-fleshed fish fillets such as sea bass or swordfish look just as good on this glowing orange sauce. Linguine or spaghetti are traditional with fish.

1 tablespoon olive oil	*1 can (7-oz.) crushed tomatoes*
1 onion, thinly sliced	*Grated zest and juice of 1½ oranges*
2 garlic cloves, minced	*Good pinch saffron strands, soaked in*
2 fennel bulbs, thinly sliced	*a little warm water*
1 teaspoon Pernod or a squeeze of lemon	*12 black olives cured in brine, rinsed*
Salt and freshly ground black pepper	*1 pound red mullet fillets, cut into 4 pieces*

Warm a large, heavy-bottomed saucepan over the stove, then add the oil. Add the onion, garlic, and fennel and cook over low heat until softened. Add the Pernod or lemon juice and season to taste with salt and pepper.

Add the tomatoes and orange zest and juice and simmer until the fennel is just tender. Stir in the saffron and its liquid and olives. Lay the fish fillets on top, cover with a tight-fitting lid, and leave the fish to "steam" for 5 to 8 minutes, depending on its thickness. Serve at once over hot pasta.

Fresh Tuna, Red Onion, and Balsamic Vinegar

Serve this with an arugula or green salad mixed with plenty of herbs, and use a pasta shape such as conchiglie to trap the onion pieces. Although tuna is a fatty fish, it contains a wealth of essential vitamins and minerals, so it can occasionally feature in low-fat diets when eaten in a small portion.

1 tablespoon olive oil	*Salt and freshly ground black pepper*
6½ cups diced red onions	*1 pound fresh tuna, cut into 4 steaks*
1 to 2 tablespoons balsamic vinegar	

Warm a large, heavy-bottomed saucepan over low heat. Add the oil and onions, stir to coat the onions in the oil, and cover the pan tightly so they cook in their own steam for about 20 minutes. Stir from time to time to prevent sticking.

When the onions are soft, stir in the vinegar and season to taste with salt and pepper. Move the onions to the side of the pan. Add the tuna steaks and cook for about 2 minutes on each side, or until the tuna is cooked through to your liking. Lift the tuna out of the pan, add the hot pasta to the pan, and toss with the onion mixture. Serve at once, topped with the tuna.

Steak, Mushroom, and Truffle Oil

Try this as a luxurious main course with pappardelle.

1 tablespoon peanut oil	*1 pound beef tenderloin or sirloin steak,*
4 shallots, minced	*cut into thin strips*
1 garlic clove, minced	*4 tablespoons beef stock*
3 cups thinly sliced button mushrooms,	*4 tablespoons Madeira or dry sherry*
Salt and freshly ground black pepper	*1 tablespoon chopped fresh parsley*
	Truffle oil for garnish

Warm a skillet over the stove; then add half the oil. Add the shallots, garlic, and mushrooms and fry until the shallots are soft. Season to taste with salt and pepper; remove from the pan and keep warm.

Turn up the heat. Add the remaining oil and stir-fry the steak for 2 to 3 minutes; transfer to the plate with the mushroom mixture.

Add the stock and Madeira or sherry to the pan and boil until it reduces by three-quarters. Return the mushroom mixture and meat to the pan and heat through briefly. Stir in the parsley. Serve over hot pasta, garnished with a few drops of truffle oil.

Right: Artichokes, Peas, and Prosciutto

MONKFISH AND ROSEMARY

Monkfish is easy to prepare and satisfying to eat. Serve with linguine.

1 tablespoon olive oil	3 or 4 sprigs fresh rosemary
1 onion, finely chopped	1 pound monkfish fillet, skinned
1 cup tomato passata (see page 8)	Salt and freshly ground black pepper

Warm a saucepan over the stove, then add the oil. Add the onion, cover with a tight-fitting lid, and cook until soft, about 10 minutes. Stir in the passata and rosemary and simmer, uncovered, for 15 to 20 minutes, until thicker.

Meanwhile, slice the monkfish into slices about 1 inch thick.

Season the tomato sauce with salt and pepper to taste. Add the monkfish and simmer for about 3 minutes until it is just tender. Serve at once over hot pasta.

VENISON, CHESTNUT, AND ORANGE

Low-fat chestnuts and oranges provide a complementary flavor and help the venison stretch farther. Serve with bretelloni or lasagnette.

1 tablespoon all-purpose flour	1 cup beef or chicken stock
Salt and freshly ground black pepper	7 ounces vacuum-packed or canned
14 ounces boneless venison, diced	unsweetened chestnuts, drained if
2 tablespoons olive oil	necessary
2 onions, thinly sliced	Grated zest and juice of 1 orange
2/3 cup dry red wine	2 teaspoons red currant or cranberry jelly

Season the flour with salt and pepper and then toss the venison in it. Warm the oil in a heatproof casserole. Add the onions and cook until soft. Move them to the side of the pan and add the venison. Seal the meat over medium-high heat. Add the wine, stock, and chestnuts. Bring to a boil, stirring constantly. Remove from the heat and stir in the orange zest and juice and the jelly. Cover with a tight-fitting lid and simmer over very low heat for about 1 hour, or until the venison is tender. Season to taste and serve over hot pasta.

VENISON, RED CURRANT, AND PORT

Look for venison at specialty butchers. It's low in fat and loaded with nutrients. Serve with rigatoni.

14 ounces ground venison	3 or 4 sprigs fresh thyme
3 shallots, minced	1 bay leaf
1 tablespoon olive oil	3/4 cup beef stock
3 cups finely chopped mushrooms	1/2 cup ruby port wine
1 garlic clove, crushed	4 tablespoons red currant jelly
1 tablespoon soy sauce	Salt and freshly ground black pepper

Put the venison, shallots, and oil in a hot saucepan, cover, and cook, stirring occasionally, for 5 minutes. Add the mushrooms, garlic, soy sauce, thyme, bay leaf, stock, and half the port wine and simmer slowly for about 20 minutes. Stir in the remaining port wine and the red currant jelly and simmer for 5 minutes longer. Season to taste with salt and pepper and serve over hot pasta.

LAMB WITH ROASTED VEGETABLES AND MINT

This is a great way to make a small amount of meat go a long way—and the colors are amazing. Serve with any small pasta—wholegrain is good—and a glass of Sangiovese wine.

8 sprigs fresh thyme or 1/2 teaspoon dried thyme	2 red onions, cut into wedges
3 garlic cloves, sliced	2 yellow bell peppers, cut into chunks
Coarsely ground black pepper	4 tomatoes, quartered
1 1/2 tablespoons olive oil	1 bunch fresh mint, shredded
2 lamb neck tenderloins, trimmed of all excess fat	Salt

Rub the thyme, garlic, pepper, and 1/2 tablespoon of the oil into the lamb. Let marinate for at least 30 minutes, or several hours in the refrigerator.

Preheat the oven to its highest setting. Put the onion wedges in a roasting pan and sprinkle with the remaining oil. Roast in the hot oven for 20 minutes.

Shake the thyme and garlic off the lamb, reserving as much as you can. Warm a heavy-bottomed skillet over the stove, then sear the meat to seal on all sides. Add to the roasting pan together with the reserved thyme and garlic, peppers, and tomatoes and roast for 20 minutes.

Remove the lamb from the pan and leave to stand for 5 minutes, then slice and return to the roasting pan. Add the mint and hot pasta to the meat and vegetables and toss so the pasta gets mixed with the cooking juices. Season to taste with salt and serve at once.

SQUID INK SAUCE

An adaptation of the Venetian dish, *risotto nero*, produces this dramatically dark sauce. Squid ink is sold in gourmet stores and by some fish merchants and supermarkets. Serve with spaghetti or linguine.

1 1/4 pounds whole squid, or 1 pound dressed squid and 1 sachet squid ink	2 tablespoons chopped fresh parsley, plus extra to garnish
1 1/2 tablespoons olive oil	2/3 cup dry white wine
3 shallots, minced	2/3 cup hot fish stock
1 garlic clove, minced	Salt and freshly ground black pepper

Clean the squid if necessary (see page 9), keeping the ink sacs separate, and cut the bodies into strips 1/4-inch wide.

Warm a heavy-bottomed saucepan over the stove, then add the oil. Add the shallots, garlic, and parsley and sauté over low heat until the shallots are tender. Add the squid, including the tentacles, and simmer for 10 minutes, stirring frequently. Add the wine and simmer for about 25 minutes longer, adding the stock a little at a time to keep the mixture moist. Just before serving, stir in the squid ink to make a black sauce. and season to taste with salt and pepper. Serve over hot pasta, garnished with parsley.

Right: Lamb with Roasted Vegetables and Mint

LIGHT BOLOGNESE

Authentic *ragù bolognese* begins by softening the vegetables in oil and butter. This recipe eliminates the butter, because the milk helps to give the sauce a creamy texture. This sauce goes well with almost any pasta, from the classic spaghetti to penne or—just for fun—rotelle.

1 tablespoon olive oil	Freshly grated nutmeg
1 onion, minced	1/2 cup low-fat or skim milk
1 carrot, finely chopped	1 can (14-oz.) crushed tomatoes
1 celery rib, minced	1 cup red or white dry wine
1 pound lean ground beef	2 sprigs fresh thyme or 1 teaspoon
Salt and freshly ground black pepper	dried thyme

Warm a heavy-bottomed saucepan over the stove, then add the oil. Add the onion, carrot, and celery, cover, and cook over low heat for 4 to 5 minutes until soft. Add the beef, turn up the heat, and break up the meat with a wooden spoon until it is no longer pink, about 2 minutes; do not overcook at this stage. Season to taste with salt, pepper, and nutmeg. Stir in the milk and simmer, stirring, until it evaporates, about 10 minutes.

Add the tomatoes, wine, and thyme and simmer, uncovered, stirring from time to time, for 1 to 1½ hours until thick. Taste and adjust the seasoning. Serve over hot pasta.

BAKED MEDITERRANEAN PASTA

This vegetarian dish is a cross between ratatouille and moussaka. Use penne or rigatoni—11 ounces should be enough for four people.

1 eggplant, cut into 3/4-inch cubes	Salt and freshly ground black pepper
1 tablespoon olive oil	1 can (14-oz.) crushed tomatoes
1 teaspoon coriander seeds, crushed with	2/3 cup low-fat plain yogurt
a mortar and pestle	1/2 cup part-skim ricotta cheese
1 teaspoon dried thyme	1/2 teaspoon Dijon mustard
1 onion, chopped	2 egg whites
3 cups sliced zucchini	
1 small red and 1 small yellow bell pepper,	
roughly chopped	

Steam the eggplant until just tender, 15 to 20 minutes. Preheat the oven to 350°F.

Meanwhile, warm a heavy-bottomed saucepan over the stove, then add the oil. Add the coriander seeds, thyme, and onion and cook until the onion is soft. Add the zucchini and bell peppers, cover the saucepan, and cook, stirring occasionally, until the vegetables begin to soften. Season generously with salt and pepper and stir in the eggplant and tomatoes. Mix with hot pasta and transfer to a baking dish.

Mix the yogurt with the ricotta cheese and season with the mustard and salt and pepper to taste. Whisk the egg whites until stiff and fold them into the yogurt mixture. Spread over the vegetable mixture. Bake for 30 to 35 minutes. Serve hot.

LAMB, APRICOT, AND CHICKPEA

This Moroccan-inspired dish can be served with gnocchetti sardi, conchiglie, or even couscous, which is, after all, made with durum wheat, like pasta.

1 tablespoon all-purpose flour	2 teaspoons ground cinnamon
Salt and freshly ground black pepper	1 teaspoon ground ginger
1 pound boneless, lean lamb, cubed	Pinch cayenne pepper
1½ tablespoons olive oil	1 cup ready-to-eat dried apricots
2 onions, minced	1 cup canned chickpeas, drained

Season the flour with salt and pepper and toss the lamb in it; set aside. Warm a heavy-bottomed saucepan over the stove, then add the oil. Add the onions and spices and cook until soft and fragrant. Move them to the side of the pan and add the lamb. Cook, stirring often, to seal the meat.

Add the apricots and just enough water to cover. Bring to simmering point, cover with a tight-fitting lid, and simmer for 20 to 30 minutes, or until the lamb is tender. Add the chickpeas and simmer for 5 minutes. Season to taste and serve over hot pasta.

RABBIT AND CHERRY

Like all small game animals, rabbit is low in fat. Depending on the size of the rabbit, and whether you use the saddle, legs, or both, this will serve four to six people. If you have time to plan ahead, use the rabbit bones to make the stock. Serve with pappardelle.

2 tablespoons olive oil	2 tablespoons all-purpose flour
1 onion, minced	2/3 cup dry red wine
1 celery rib, minced	1 cinnamon stick
1 rabbit (see above), boned and cut	About 1 cup hot rabbit or beef stock
into 3/4-inch cubes	4 ounces morello cherries in natural juice or
2 or 3 sprigs fresh thyme	light syrup, drained
Salt and freshly ground black pepper	

Warm a heavy-bottomed saucepan over the stove, reduce the heat to low and add the oil. Add the onion and celery and cook until soft. Turn up the heat, add the meat, and brown all over. Add the thyme, salt and pepper to taste, and flour and stir for 2 to 3 minutes. Add the wine and cinnamon and continue cooking over low heat, stirring often, until almost all the liquid evaporates.

Pour in enough hot stock just to cover the meat. Cover the pan and leave to simmer very slowly for 1 to 2 hours, depending on the age of the rabbit, adding more stock a little at a time to keep the mixture moist. When the rabbit is tender and the sauce is thick, stir in the cherries and adjust the seasoning to taste. Toss with hot pasta and serve at once.

NOTE

Cherries in natural juice can be difficult to find; I used a Turkish brand of cherries in syrup with a pleasantly tart flavor. Taste the cherries before you add them; if they are too sweet, rinse them and add a squeeze of lemon juice to the sauce.

Right: *Light Bolognese*

PASTA AL FRESCO

Cold pasta dishes, like most other salads, should ideally be made as soon as possible before serving. Cook the pasta and drain well, then toss thoroughly with a tablespoon of olive oil and leave to cool. When cold, it is ready to use in one of the following recipes.

SMOKY EGGPLANT SAUCE

You need gas burners on your stovetop for this, or you can use a small hand-held burner if you put the eggplants on a heatproof plate—and you will wonder what's going on as the eggplant skin falls off in little black flakes. Don't worry—it's easy to clean up and the smoky flavor of this almost fat-free sauce is out of this world. It is good with casareccie.

2 eggplants
2 tablespoons lemon juice
Salt and freshly ground black pepper
4 tablespoons plain yogurt
Good pinch of dried oregano
Good pinch of dried thyme
5 or 6 tablespoons finely chopped fresh parsley

Place the eggplants directly over the gas burners and "roast" in the flames for 5 to 10 minutes, turning frequently (use spoons) until soft. Leave until cool enough to handle, then scrape off the burned skin. Cut the stem end off, then chop and mash the eggplant to make a rough puree. Add the lemon juice, salt, and plenty of pepper.

Mix the yogurt, oregano, and thyme together. Season to taste with salt and pepper and mix with the eggplant puree. Finally, stir in the parsley and cold pasta.

SALMON BLOODY MARY

Serve this spicy salad as a first course to kick start the tastebuds, using about 8 ounces pasta for four people. Choose radiatore, rotelle, or fusilli bucati.

4 tablespoons vodka
3/4 cup tomato passata (see page 8)
2 to 3 teaspoons Worcestershire sauce
1 to 2 dashes hot pepper sauce
Juice of 1/2 to 1 lemon
Celery salt and freshly ground black pepper
8 ounces smoked salmon, cut into thin strips
4 leafy tops of celery ribs, to garnish

Mix the vodka and passata with the Worcestershire and hot pepper sauces and lemon juice. Season with celery salt and pepper; taste and adjust the seasonings.

Stir in the smoked salmon and cold pasta. Serve each portion garnished with a small rib of leafy celery.

TURKEY AND TARRAGON WITH POMEGRANATE SEEDS

Here's a special way to brighten up leftover turkey. Serve with mixed green and white fusilli.

1 cup low-fat plain yogurt
1/2 cup walnuts, finely chopped
1 garlic clove, crushed
4 sprigs fresh tarragon, leaves stripped and finely chopped
1 teaspoon coarse mustard
Salt and freshly ground black pepper
3 cups skinless cooked turkey, cut into slivers
1 pomegranate

Combine the yogurt, walnuts, garlic, tarragon, and mustard. Season to taste with salt and pepper. Stir in the turkey.

Cut the pomegranate in half and extract the jewel-like seeds from the bitter white membrane.

Serve the turkey salad on a bed of cold pasta and scatter the pomegranate seeds over the top.

THAI-STYLE CHICKEN SALAD

Thai noodle salads are traditionally made with wiry soybean flour noodles called *wun sen*. Vermicelli or capelli d'angelo are the closest wheat flour alternative. In Thailand, these salads are often numbingly hot with chilies—use the smaller amount unless you have built up your chili tolerance level.

9 ounces chicken, minced
2 tablespoons prepared Thai fish sauce, or more if needed
2 tablespoons fresh lime juice, or more if needed
1 or 2 small fresh chilies, minced, or 1/2 to 1 tablespoon prepared sweet chili sauce
1 teaspoon light brown sugar, or more if needed
2-inch piece peeled fresh ginger, finely shredded
1 small mango or papaya, peeled and cubed
8 canned water chestnuts, chopped
Large handful fresh basil leaves
Large handful fresh cilantro leaves
Large handful fresh mint leaves
4 large Romaine or Iceberg lettuce leaves

Warm a wok or heavy-bottomed skillet over medium-high heat. Add the chicken, fish sauce, lime juice, chilies, and sugar and cook, stirring to break up the meat, for 8 to 10 minutes, or until the chicken is cooked through; leave to cool.

Stir in the ginger, fruit, and water chestnuts. Taste and add more fish sauce, lime juice, or sugar as required. Mix with the herbs and cold pasta. Pour the mixture onto the lettuce leaves and serve at once.

Fresh Herb Sauce

The glorious emerald green of this sauce should remind you that it's packed with vitamins and minerals. Serve with conchiglie.

1 tablespoon fresh tarragon leaves	Flesh of ½ avocado
4 tablespoons fresh parsley leaves	6 tablespoons low-fat plain yogurt
2 tablespoons snipped fresh chives	Salt
Generous 1 ounce watercress	2 tablespoons chopped pistachio nuts
7 tablespoons vegetable stock	(optional)

Put the herbs, stock, avocado and yogurt into a blender and blend until smooth. Add salt to taste.

Toss with cold pasta and garnish with the chopped pistachios, if using.

Hummus, Red Pepper, and Olive

This is delicious served on a bed of arugula—or serve a big green herb salad and a tomato and basil salad alongside. Fusilli is a good shape to use.

1 cup prepared hummus	4 tablespoons sliced Spanish olives
1 to 2 tablespoons lemon juice	Salt and freshly ground black pepper
1 large red bell pepper, roasted, skinned	2 tablespoons chopped fresh parsley
(see page 9), and cut into strips	

Mix the hummus with 1 tablespoon of the lemon juice, then taste and add more lemon if necessary. Stir in all the remaining ingredients together with cold pasta and serve.

Cauliflower, Red Pepper, Black Olive, and Feta

This tasty variation on a Greek salad makes a main course for four but feeds more if served as a first course or accompaniment. Use spinach-flavored fusilli or orecchiette.

½ cauliflower, cut into florets	4 tomatoes, skinned, seeded (see page 9),
1 tablespoon olive oil	and diced
2 teaspoons lemon juice	½ cup crumbled feta cheese
Salt and freshly ground black pepper	¾ cup rinsed, pitted, and halved olives
2 scallions, minced	cured in brine
2 red bell peppers, roasted, skinned	
(see page 9), and cut into strips	

Blanch the cauliflower in boiling water for 2 to 3 minutes; drain and rinse in cold water. Drain well and mix with the olive oil, lemon juice, salt, pepper, and scallions.

Stir in the remaining ingredients and toss with cold pasta.

Smoked Trout and Dill

Palest pink with flecks of green; this pretty pasta salad looks good when made with farfalle.

8 ounces smoked trout, cut into strips	Salt and freshly ground black pepper
½ lemon	1¾ cups low-fat plain yogurt
2 tablespoons chopped fresh dill	1 teaspoon coarse mustard

Put the smoked trout in a large bowl and add a good squeeze of lemon juice plus the dill and salt and pepper to taste. Gently stir in the yogurt, mustard, and cold pasta.

Shrimp and Asparagus in Light Pesto

A light, luxury-class first-course salad. Choose pasta shells or fusilli. For additional flavor, use the asparagus cooking water to cook the pasta.

6 ounces asparagus tips	6 ounces cooked tiger prawns or jumbo
4 to 6 teaspoons prepared pesto	shrimp
4 to 6 tablespoons low-fat plain yogurt	

Cook the asparagus in a large saucepan of boiling water for 2 to 3 minutes until just tender. Drain, refresh in cold water, and drain well again. Cut into 1-inch pieces on the diagonal.

Mix the pesto with the yogurt. Stir in the cold pasta. Gently stir in the prawns or shrimp and asparagus. Serve at once.

Right: Fresh Herb Sauce

ROASTED PEPPERS WITH ANCHOVY AND OLIVE

The typical Italian salad: classic, simple, vibrantly colored and flavored. Serve with penne.

2 red, 2 yellow, and 2 green bell peppers, roasted, skinned (see page 9), and cut into ¹/2-inch strips

2 (2-oz.) cans anchovy fillets, drained and rinsed (see page 7)

³/4 cup rinsed and pitted black olives, cured in brine

Salt and freshly ground black pepper

2 tablespoons chopped fresh parsley

Put the pepper strips into a bowl together with their juices, the anchovies, and olives. Toss with cold pasta. Season to taste with salt and pepper and garnish with the parsley.

EGGPLANT AND TOMATO SALSA WITH PINE NUTS

Salting and steaming the eggplants make them meltingly tender without the need for oil. The vegetables and nuts nestle perfectly inside conchiglie.

2 eggplants, cut into ¹/2-inch cubes

Salt and freshly ground black pepper

2 pounds ripe tomatoes, cut into ¹/2-inch cubes (about 6 cups)

1 red onion, minced

2 garlic cloves, chopped

¹/2 cup pine nuts, toasted

Large bunch fresh basil, roughly chopped

4 tablespoons finely chopped fresh parsley

1 teaspoon sugar (optional)

Put the eggplant cubes in a colander and sprinkle with plenty of salt. Leave for 20 to 30 minutes. Rinse the eggplant well, pat dry on paper towels, and return to the colander or place in a steamer. Cover and steam for 15 to 20 minutes, or until tender; let cool.

In a large bowl, gently mix the eggplant with the remaining ingredients, adding sugar and salt and pepper to taste. Toss with cold pasta.

AVOCADO SALSA

This colorful salsa looks very pretty with farfalle.

5 tomatoes, seeded and diced

1 bunch scallions, finely sliced

2 garlic cloves, minced

Handful fresh cilantro, roughly chopped

Dash hot pepper sauce

3 avocados, peeled, pitted, and cut into ¹/2-inch dice

Juice of 2 limes

Salt and freshly ground black pepper

Mix the tomatoes, scallions, garlic, cilantro, and hot pepper sauce together. Gently toss the avocados with the lime juice and salt and pepper to taste. Combine with the tomato mixture and cold pasta.

GREEN BEANS WITH ROASTED TOMATO AND BASIL SAUCE

Serve this simple salad with broiled fish or meat, or as part of a buffet with other salads. Penne rigate is the pasta of choice for this salad.

1 teaspoon olive oil

5 tomatoes

4 garlic cloves, unpeeled

12 ounces green beans

Salt and freshly ground black pepper

Handful fresh basil leaves, finely shredded

¹/2 small red onion, very thinly sliced

A few fresh basil leaves to garnish

Preheat the oven to 400°F. Brush the oil over a cooking sheet. Add the whole tomatoes and garlic cloves and roast for 20 to 30 minutes until the tomatoes begin to shrivel.

Meanwhile, cook the green beans in boiling water until just tender; drain and refresh in cold water. Drain well and cut diagonally into 1½-inch pieces.

Peel the garlic cloves. Rub the tomatoes and garlic through a nylon strainer over a large bowl. Season to taste with salt and pepper and stir in the shredded basil. Toss with the green beans, onion, and cold pasta. Serve garnished with basil leaves.

Right: Roasted Peppers with Anchovy and Olive

PASTA NIÇOISE

A classic main-course salad for a summer day. The green beans look best with penne or a similarly shaped pasta.

12 ounces green beans	*Salt and freshly ground black pepper*
1 can (7-oz.) tuna in water, well drained	*3/4 cup pitted black olives cured in brine*
1/2 cup low-fat plain yogurt	*1 can (2-oz.) anchovy fillets, rinsed*
1 garlic clove, crushed	*and dried (see page 7)*
1/2 red and 1/2 green bell peppers, cut	*4 hard-boiled eggs, halved*
into 1/2-inch squares	*4 tomatoes, quartered*
1/2 tablespoon capers, drained (optional)	

Cook the green beans in boiling water until just tender. Drain well, refresh in cold water, and drain again; set aside.

Mix the tuna with the yogurt, garlic, peppers, and capers, if using. Season to taste with salt and pepper.

Mix the green beans with the cold pasta and the olives. Season to taste with salt and pepper. Spoon onto a plate and spoon the tuna mixture into the middle. Arrange the anchovies, eggs, and tomatoes over the salad.

MILDLY CURRIED CHICKEN

Fusilli is a good choice of pasta for this dish.

1 small chicken, quartered	*3 tablespoons mango chutney*
1 tablespoon peanut oil	*6 tablespoons low-fat plain yogurt*
1 onion, minced	*2 tablespoons golden raisins*
1 apple, cored, peeled, and diced	*Freshly ground black pepper*
1 tablespoon mild curry paste	

TO GARNISH:

2 tablespoons slivered almonds, toasted	*2 tablespoons roughly chopped fresh*
Pinch paprika	*cilantro*

Put the chicken pieces into a saucepan. Add just enough water to cover and bring to the boil. Cover, lower the heat, and simmer for 20 to 30 minutes until cooked through. Let cool in the liquid. Lift out the chicken and cut the meat into slivers; discard the skin and bones, but reserve the chicken cooking liquid.

Heat the oil in a saucepan. Add the onion and apple and cook until soft. Stir in the curry paste and 1/2 cup of the chicken cooking liquid and simmer for 2 minutes. Puree with the mango chutney until smooth, adding a little more chicken cooking liquid if necessary. Let cool in a bowl.

Stir in the yogurt, chicken, golden raisins, and cold pasta. Season to taste with pepper. Sprinkle with the slivered almonds, dust with paprika, and garnish with the cilantro.

CHARGRILLED SALMON WITH OLIVE SALSA

This is a main-course salad full of bold flavors that can be served either hot or cold. If, despite careful turning, the salmon skin detaches itself, don't worry—cut it into strips and scatter over the salmon to get the benefit of the smoky flavor. Try this with spaghetti, radiatore, or fusilli.

FOR THE OLIVE SALSA:

3/4 cup rinsed, pitted, and finely chopped	*4 large tomatoes, skinned, seeded*
black olives, cured in brine	*(see page 9), and diced*
3/4 cup rinsed, pitted, and finely chopped	*3 tablespoons chopped fresh cilantro*
Spanish olives, cured in brine	*Juice of 1 lime*
1 fresh chili, minced	*Salt and freshly ground black pepper*

FOR THE SALAD:

A little olive oil for brushing	*Salt and freshly ground black pepper*
Four 5-ounce salmon fillets with skin,	*4 sprigs fresh cilantro, to garnish*
scaled	*1 lime, cut into quarters, to garnish*

Mix together all the ingredients for the salsa, adding salt and pepper to taste.

Heat a grill pan until very hot and brush with oil. Add the salmon, skin-side down, and cook for 2 to 3 minutes. Turn carefully and cook the other side for 1 to 2 minutes. (Cook the salmon for longer if you like; these timings set up a contrast between the blackened outside and very lightly cooked middle.) Season to taste with salt and pepper.

To serve, spoon the salsa onto a bed of cold pasta. Add a salmon fillet, skin-side up. Top with a sprig of cilantro and serve with a lime wedge to squeeze over the salmon.

Right: Pasta Niçoise

RECIPE INDEX

mussels:
   Mixed Seafood 44
   Mussels, Fennel, and Pernod 42
   Mussels Masala 37
   Mussels and Saffron 24

Niçoise, Pasta 60

olives:
   Cauliflower, Red Pepper, Black
      Olive, and Feta 56
   Chargrilled Asparagus with
      Spanish Olives and Basil 29
   Chargrilled Salmon with Olive
      Salsa 60
   Hummus, Red Pepper, and
      Olive 56
   Pasta Niçoise 60
   Roasted Peppers with
      Anchovy and Olive 58
onions:
   Chargrilled Leek and Red
      Onion, with Salsa Verde 32
   Fresh Tuna, Red Onion, and
      Balsamic Vinegar 48
   Golden Onion and Anchovy
      14
   Lamb with Roasted Vegetables
      and Mint 50
   Liver Veneziana 44
   Pearl Onion Curry 36

Paprika Chicken 20
Paprika Pork 46
peas:
   Artichokes, Peas, and Prosciutto
      48
   Lamb and Mint Pesto 14
   Zucchini and Mint 26
peppers, bell:
   Baked Mediterranean Pasta 52
   Broccoli and Hot Red Pepper
      34
   Cauliflower, Red Pepper, Black
      Olive, and Feta 56
   Fish with Pimentos, Pine Nuts,
      and Parsley 14
   Five-Spice Lamb 36
   Hummus, Red Pepper, and
      Olive 56
   Lamb with Roasted Vegetables
      and Mint 50
   Pasta Niçoise 60
   Roasted Peppers with
      Anchovy and Olive 58
   Roasted Vegetable 28
   Spicy Moroccan Eggplant 38

Tomato-Curry Sauce with
   Smoked Tofu 38
Vegetable Spaghetti 32
pine nuts:
   Eggplant and Tomato Salsa
      with Pine Nuts 58
   Fish with Pimentos, Pine
      Nuts, and Parsley 14
   Lemon and Pine Nut with
      Thyme Gremolata 30
   Pasta con le Sarde 44
   Vegetable Spaghetti 32
pork:
   Paprika Pork 46
   Pork, Pineapple, and Cilantro
      41
potato(es):
   and Garlic with Caviar 22
   Sweet Potato and Broccoli 33
pumpkin:
   Pumpkin with Dates,
      Chickpeas, and Saffron 46
   Roasted Pumpkin and Sage 33

Rabbit and Cherry 52
Red Mullet with Fennel and
   Orange 48
Roasted Pepper with Anchovy
   and Olive 58
Roasted Pumpkin and Sage 33
Roasted Roots with Lassi 46
Roasted Tomato and Garlic 29
Roasted Vegetable 28
Rosemary Chicken 20

Saffron Chicken and Shrimp 46
salmon:
   Chargrilled Salmon with Olive
      Salsa 60
   Salmon Bloody Mary 54
   Salmon with Soy, Mustard, and
      Dill 42
   Salmon Teriyaki 24
sardines:
   Pasta con le Sarde 44
scallops:
   Scallops and Lime 14
   Scallops with Spicy Leeks 16
Seafood, Mixed 44
shellfish see *name of seafood*
Smoked Chicken and Leek with
   Coarse Mustard 16

shrimp:
   Fennel and Shrimp 18
   Hot Shrimp with Basil 40
   Mixed Seafood 44

Saffron Chicken and Shrimp 46
Shrimp and Asparagus in Light
   Pesto 56
Smoked Haddock and Spinach 16
Smoked Trout and Dill 56
Smoky Eggplant Sauce 54
squid:
   Chargrilled Squid with Sesame
      Dressing 18
   Mixed Seafood 44
   Squid Ink Sauce 50
   Squid with Lemongrass 40
   Squid Provençale 18
spinach:
   Mushroom, Spinach, and
      Ricotta 33
   Smoked Haddock and
      Spinach 16
   Spicy Spinach and Lentil 30
   Wilted Spinach with Fava
      Beans and Pancetta 22
Steak, Mushroom, and Truffle Oil
   48
Sweet Potato and Broccoli 33

Thai-style Chicken Salad 54
tomatoes (canned):
   Baked Mediterranean Pasta 52
   Beef and Mushoom 18
   Black Bean and Tomato 34
   Cajun Chicken 42
   Chicken Chili with Chickpeas
      41
   Light Bolognese 52
   Red Mullet with Fennel and
      Orange 48
   Rich Tomato and Oregano 26
   Squid Provençale 18
   Tomato-Macaroni Gratin 30
   Tuna Pizzaiola 24
tomatoes (fresh):
   Avocado Salsa 58
   Broccoli and Hot Red Pepper
      34
   Cauliflower, Red Pepper, Black
      Olive, and Feta 60
   Chargrilled Salmon with Olive
      Salsa 60
   Eggplant and Tomato Salsa
      with Pine Nuts 58
   Fresh Tomato and Basil 26
   Green Beans with Roasted
      Tomato and Basil Sauce 58
   Lamb with Roasted Vegetables
      and Mint 50
   Mixed Seafood 44
   Paprika Pork 46

Pasta Niçoise 60
Roasted Corn and Zucchini
   Salsa 34
Roasted Pumpkin and Sage 33
Roasted Tomato and Garlic 29
Saffron Chicken and Shrimp 46
Tomato-Curry Sauce with
   Smoked Tofu 38
tuna:
   Fresh Tuna, Red Onion, and
      Balsamic Vinegar 48
   Pasta Niçoise 60
   Tuna Pizzaiola 24
turkey:
   Turkey, Prosciutto, and Sage 20
   Turkey and Tarragon with
      Pomegranate Seeds 54
Tuscan Chicken Liver Sauce 16

Vegetable Spaghetti 32
Venison, Chestnut, and Orange
   50
Venison, Red Currant, and Port
   50

watercress:
   Fresh Herb Sauce 56
   Wilted Spinach with Fava Beans
      and Pancetta 22

zucchini:
   Baked Mediterranean Pasta 52
   Roasted Corn and Zucchini
      Salsa 34
   Roasted Vegetable 28
   Zucchini and Mint 26

ACKNOWLEDGMENTS

I would like to thank Susan Haynes and Laura Washburn for all their support and good humour.
Laura had a hand in making this book look so good, too, for which I am also very grateful to
Robin Matthews, stylist Roisin Nield, and home economist Emma Patmore.
For nurturing my tastebuds and letting me into their kitchens at an early age I bless Grandma
and thank my parents. For being there for me, caring, sharing friends come no better than
Helen Roylance, and I also thank her husband, Paul Brown, for that manly shoulder. Ian Chilvers
has kept my spirits up with a constant stream of presents, and inspiration and recipes have
been generously given by Julia Gregory, Lydia Roberts, and Robert Saxton. Above all, for their
kind and practical help in the kitchen, the market, and the ideas department, I thank Andrew
Thompson (without whom this book would not have happened) and his father, Tommy.

First published in the United States of America in 1999 by

Rizzoli International Publications, Inc.

300 Park Avenue South, New York, NY 10010

First published in Great Britain in 1999 by

George Weidenfeld and Nicolson Limited

The Orion Publishing Group

Orion House

5 Upper St. Martin's Lane

London WC2H 9EA

Text copyright © Weidenfeld & Nicolson 1999

Photographs © Robin Matthews

ISBN 0-8478-2188-9

LC 98-68194

Printed in Italy